THE POEM

Renata Ferreira

THE POEMS OF

Renata Ferreira

TRANSCRIBED AND ANNOTATED,
WITH A FOREWORD BY

FRANK X. GASPAR

TAGUS PRESS
UNIVERSITY OF MASSACHUSETTS DARTMOUTH
DARTMOUTH, MA

Tagus Press is the publishing arm of the
Center for Portuguese Studies and Culture at
the University of Massachusetts Dartmouth.
Center Director: Victor K. Mendes

Portuguese in the Americas 26
Tagus Press at the University of Massachusetts Dartmouth
© 2020 Frank X. Gaspar

Executive Editor: Mario Pereira
Series Editors: Christopher Larkosh & Gloria de Sá
Copyedited by Dawn Potter and Sharon Brinkman
Designed and typeset by adam b. bohannon

For all inquiries, please contact:
Tagus Press
Center for Portuguese Studies and Culture
University of Massachusetts Dartmouth
285 Old Westport Road
North Dartmouth MA 02747–2300
(508) 999-8255, fax (508) 999-9272
https://www.umassd.edu/portuguese-studies-center/

ISBN: 978-1-933227-94-8
Library of Congress control number: 2019953874

FOR MARY, WITH ABIDING LOVE.

CONTENTS

ACKNOWLEDGMENTS

My sincere thanks to my dear friends in Lisbon, Professors Teresa Alves and Margarida Vale de Gato, for their enthusiastic and helpful readings of Renata's poems.

My thanks also to Ellen Bass for her committed and sensitive reading and ongoing encouragement for this project, as well as for her friendship, counsel, and good humor.

Additionally, my gratitude to Mario Pereira, Executive Editor of Tagus Press, for his patience with my deadlines and queries, and for his stalwart support with logistical issues large and small.

I would especially like to thank the irrepresible Christopher Larkosh, former Director of Tagus Press and Editor for the book series in which this book is published, for his robust interest in Renata's poems, his apt suggestions, his good cheer, and his vigorous shepherding of the book through the highways and back-streets of its production. He has been a vital force in bringing Renata's work into the light.

And finally, my profound thanks to Mary Oliver, whose enduring friendship has been a blessing over the decades, from my first book to the final draft of this collection of Renata's poems.

I.

Renata Ferreira emerges from a past freighted with well-documented historical events, but accounts of her personal life include many gaps and a good deal of uncertainty in the telling, and her biography may always remain incomplete. What we do know depends on particular recollections from several personal sources (some second- and thirdhand), my own notes, and the poems themselves. Because I knew Renata when I was a child and teenager in Provincetown, where she summered in the late '50s and early '60s, and then later in New York City in 1965 and 1966, and because the only known manuscript of her poems came to me in the extraordinary manner that it did, I find that I cannot extricate myself from the narrative of her life as we know it.

In the summers, Renata lived in the old West End of Provincetown as a roomer in our house, and sometimes with the Bento family, whose house sat at the bottom of Franklin Street, catercorner to ours. I remember Renata living in the small bedroom that our neighbor Margaret Bento had made available by moving her daughter Ana in with her older sister Rosa, making them uneasy roommates for three months. We had an attic where two young men from New York stayed with us pretty regularly, so when Renata stayed at our house, she took the one spare room in the corner. It was where we stored a lot of boxes and odds and ends in the winter. In summer we outfitted it as a bedroom, and I remember my mother and grandfather carrying things out to the shed, and then bringing other things in from the shed and putting an iron bedframe together and setting up the room. There was a tall cardboard wardrobe against one wall where Renata kept her clothes. Other than the bed and the wardrobe, Renata kept a red wooden chair and a table that always had books on it. Ana Bento and I were the same age, about eight years old, and spent a lot of time at one house or another. We had a bond, even then, that would become important later to these accounts.

Provincetown was historically divided east and west by a rail line that once crossed Commercial Street at the town wharf and proceeded to the end of it. Now named MacMillan Pier, it was referred to as "Railroad Wharf" when we were kids. *Our* West End began at about Grozier's Park, a small field and seawall where the Boatslip Hotel now stands. The town had an older, gentler look then. There were still three elms on our corner where Franklin Street and Tremont Street joined Commercial Street, just where it angled left at ninety degrees and ran by the little firehouse for Engine Number One. Adjacent to the firehouse was the three-story weathering hulk of the Atlantic Coast Fisheries plant, which was simply known as the Cold Storage, the two words running together as one. There the street hooked west once again to run along the harbor past a boatyard and out to the edge of town where a rugged breakwater extended to that part of Long Point that we called Wood End, where an abandoned coast guard station rose solitary in the distance among small hummocks of beach grass. In our part of town there were big oaks and chestnut trees on Tremont and Franklin streets, and the streets were narrow and the houses snugged together along them. People could lean on their gates or behind their hedges and talk to one another, and it was not unusual for women to hail one another at a distance and converse by yelling, most often in two languages at once.

Our neighborhood was Portuguese, as was most of the town, but we seemed to be a bit poorer, a bit more uneven around the edges than those in the East End, where boat captains, shop owners, and others with steady incomes lived. Although summer people, or "people from away" as we affectionally called them, lived plentifully with us, I should note that in our neighborhood there were no large or elegant guest houses. The West End in those days looked very little like it does today. Rather, all the roomers that came to our neighborhood lived pretty much as Renata did, in small and roughly kept homes, in spare rooms or unfinished attics and sometimes converted boat sheds. This was a time when a genteel bohemia was still possible. Many of our guests were gay; many were artists, teachers, writers, musicians, intellectuals, beachcombers, lovers of what in those days seemed to be an idyllic summer life. The season was a relatively easy time for us Portuguese too. I know now that the rents we charged were next to nothing, but nonetheless the extra money was laid away to stave off the misery of the winter months, with their lack of work and with oil and coal bills piling on.

There was a modest happiness to the idea that this revenue was coming in. I could read it in my mother's face and in Mrs. Bento's energetic movements. They liked having the people from away stay with us. Our roomers decorated our lives with stories and with just their very difference from us. I would call that difference *sophistication* or *worldliness* now. Then it was an unnamable fascination. They enjoyed being around us, too. They ate our Portuguese cooking, and they talked and questioned us as though we were the most interesting people on earth. Everyone seemed to think it was fun to learn Portuguese names and even some words and phrases. Renata, of course, was fluent, and very popular. She

3

told us how she and her mother, Elena, had fled to the United States in 1939 when Renata was four, to escape the escalating tensions in Europe, and specifically the oppressive regime in Portugal. She told many stories about the Azores and Lisbon, where she had recently traveled when she worked in the marine supply business. There was nothing afloat that Renata did not know about from bow to stern, and she spent a lot of time talking with fishermen and men at the boatyards. They liked that she could speak Portuguese, and even more, they liked that she could sail.

Most of the families in our neighborhood were from the island of Pico, but some were from São Miguel and some were from Flores. Renata's storytelling gave us beautiful, lush pictures of the islands, and sometimes the parents and the *velhos* and *velhas* would shed tears, overcome with *saudades*. Sometimes she would move the Portuguese vocabulary out of the range of Ana's and my understanding and there would be bawdy laughter, but we were used to this. Often the grown-ups would use Portuguese as a kind of code when they wanted to talk about some piece of gossip or scandal. But we learned how to swear and curse long before they caught on.

When Renata got into teasing back and forth with the fishermen and the Cold Storage workers, she would crack them up. She was their darling (pronounced "dahlin," of course). And she would have hilarious shouting conversations with both Mrs. Bento and my mother. I cannot speak for Mrs. Bento, but in my mother's case, the shouting would begin when Renata did not recognize the word or words my mother was pronouncing. My mother, at four feet, eleven inches tall, would pull herself up on her toes and simply start talking louder (she accused Renata of having *high talk*, meaning she did not speak with the accent nor use the idioms of Azorean-New England-Provincetown Portu-

4

guese). To be fair my mother used words I have never heard or read since. Renata would sometimes cook with my mother or Mrs. Bento, and Richard and Lew, "the boys from upstairs," as my mother called our own roomers, were constantly in and out of the kitchen, adding things to the table—bread, fruit, wine, fresh berries from the woods—especially when she stuffed sea clams with *linguiça* or made mackerel *vinha d'alhos*.

Ana and I were both somewhat silly around Renata. She was tall and dark with curly black hair cut very short, and she wore blue jeans and blue chambray work shirts and smoked Camel cigarettes, no filter. There was always a pack under the left-hand flap of her shirt. Her eyes were deep brown flecked with something lighter—almost a yellow, almost a green, almost not there at all. Her mouth was small, but her lips were full and her body was slender, boyish, and strong. Ana and I were pretty much in love with her. Renata liked us—we could tell because she liked to tease us about how Ana and I would comb the town beaches for soda bottles at the end of the day and turn them in to the little neighborhood A&P store for the deposits. She said we were capitalists but never explained herself. She called Ana, *Ana Banana,* but her name for me was simply *Coitadinho,* Portuguese for "poor little thing," a name she never abandoned, though later when I was older, she shortened it by dropping the diminutive. We all knew the roomers in our neighborhood, but Renata was another order of being. Renata was from away, but Renata was an American and she was Portuguese, too. She even *came* from Portugal.

We knew Renata was an artist and that the men from the Cold Storage would give her wooden packing boxes for her work, but as kids we never saw what she did with them or where her studio was. She did take us beachcombing a lot, and we helped her, picking through things she would use for her art—old clay pipes near the wharves where sailors had dropped them during the time of sailing ships, medicine bottles fogged or bleached by the sun, gray pieces of driftwood, bits of sea glass, even skate eggs, also called mermaid's purses. One summer we were collecting quahog shells in a net onion bag for one of her projects. The next day Renata came out with a tin tray of paints, some brushes, and a shoe box with some of the shells we had collected. She had way more than enough for herself, she told us, and then proceeded to show us how to paint them. We made little lighthouses and fishing boats on them. Then she got a big fish box from the Cold Storage and set it up for us on the sidewalk just where Commercial Street bends around the corner. "Make a sign," she said. We did. *Art Shells, 10 cents.* In memory it seems that Renata spent a lot of time with us in those days, but the art lesson has stayed with me with a special clarity. Renata was patient and precise, and she made a few boats and lighthouses with us first, explaining what she was doing and how she was looking at them. She spoke as though she were telling us important secrets. She told us that how you looked at objects was the most important thing. She kept her voice soft and clear, and I still remember how I could hear her breathing.

Our projects weren't bad. The colors were bright and bold on the little shells, and a few summer people bought some of them. It would not be the last time Renata would teach me something. Actually, she had been teaching me things from the very start. Just by being around her, listening to her talk, watching how she got along with others, I was learning that "away" was a big world full of all the things that I had only seen in pictures or read about in books, and I was learning that that was where I wanted to be.

I understand that the picture I offer of our neighborhood in that time past is probably tinted with a rosy nostalgia, and in balance

I must say there was another side to our lives, another story to the West End, and Renata understood it somehow. Maybe she had intuitions just from watching the men as they walked from their houses down Franklin and Commercial and Tremont to the Cold Storage when the whistle on the firehouse blew, signaling their lunch hour was over. A slow march. These men would never go anywhere beyond the town; they would never have any other work than this. There was something dangerous and deadening about the town as much as there was natural beauty. The men in the packing houses had jobs until winter. Few boats went out in the cold months, and men went every week to the Center Schoolhouse on Bradford Street and "signed up." This was the small unemployment payment from the state. My mother worried about money.

No one ever laughed, no one talked. Sometimes in winter I would have to go to the town wharf with a tin bucket and ask for fish from the one or two boats that still went out in the freezing weather and set their drags for flounder. Sometimes we ate eggs and onions for days. The house was cold. There was no hot running water. Mornings I could see the steam of my breath as I lay under layers of quilts. This all was a universe away from the summers. And Renata understood. The time she spent with me was about that. I am tempted to say I knew that then, but I am looking back and maybe the case is that I just know it now. She was not a do-gooder. She didn't have a savior complex. She simply realized how important she was to me, and she respected that. It was a rare and affecting force in my life.

Better days would come. At fifteen I was old enough for a state work permit. I could rack up long hours in the summer and put money by for the winter—warm clothes, school lunches, a little pocket money. Everything was completely on my own now, and nothing came out of the household. My mother found a year-round job working for the town, and a new man came on the scene, an older guy named Antone who spent money to make my mother comfortable. The house was spruced up, there was hot water plumbing, an oil furnace, and new shingles. Antone drank a lot, but he was a jovial drunk and he would bring pals over to play whist and hang around. My mother loved it. They were happy with their agreements. My mother was happy. I just knew I would get out of their way as soon as I could.

As we got older, Ana Bento and I became sweethearts and then lovers, and during the final two summers we spent in Provincetown—our last two years of high school—we both worked downtown, she at the Lobster Pot and I at the hotdog stand at the foot of the wharf. The summer town at night was carnival. Commercial Street, that narrowest of main streets, would begin to fill with traffic—foot traffic; a car could only pass in its one direction east to west with great hazard on summer nights. Beginning at about ten or eleven at night, the crowding swelled and then swelled again when the bars let out. People filled the streets until about three in the morning when the crowd thinned to singles and couples or threes making their way beneath the dim streetlights, heading to who knows where or what. The benches and sidewalk that lined the town hall grounds on the south and east edges would sometimes be jammed two and three people deep, boys, girls, men, women, all cruising, all looking to hook up, or buy dope, or if not twenty-one, find someone to buy liquor for a small negotiation. The area was known as the Meat Rack, and it seems to have not changed at all over the years. It was like a pulsing heart.

Ana and I both finished work at eleven, and walking out on the street was like walking into a party. There was never a thought of going home. We would get caught up in the swirl and drift through the revelers, meet people, smoke weed, cruise the Meat Rack just for some fun or adventure, then we would make love under a big seining skiff that had been overturned on an empty part of the beach.

We saw Renata a lot too. We looked at a show of hers in one of the East End galleries. There were boxes of all sizes, and objects inside them, framed by them. The boxes themselves were covered in designs of heavy bright paint. Often Renata and I would trade shirts, and we both used my bicycle to get around through the summer crowds. She would give me tips on how to be cool, on what kind of clothes to buy, and how to wear them. I began to feel like a summer person, and I liked it. Ana and I smoked pot with her sometimes, or drank a beer now and then up in the Catholic cemetery, where no one was likely to find us. Also, Renata could borrow a sailboat from the boatyard whenever she wanted, a little weasel, green, with yellow and red trim, and whenever the three of us found time together we would cruise the harbor in it. On good days we would sail around the back side of Long Point and skinny-dip in the warm shoals. When the tide was right, I would dive for sea clams, and either my mother would stuff them or Mrs. Bento would make a pie. It was Renata who, when we told her about spending our nights under the skiff, said something about our being idiots and the next night found us and gave us a box of condoms, which we called rubbers then. We knew Renata was seeing someone down the East End, where she stayed each summer now, but she'd often be out and about with a number of girls and we didn't really know anything about who her lovers were.

Just after Labor Day, in my last summer, the town began boarding up for winter. I was putting shutters up on the hotdog stand when Santos de Melo, a town guy a couple of years older than I was, stopped to have a cigarette and talk. He was a mess, terribly depressed, didn't know what to do. He told me how he had been drafted and had to report to the draft facility in Boston's South Station. "People are getting fucking killed over there," he said. He was talking about Vietnam. Everyone was talking about Vietnam now, though no one had really heard of it before. Town guys were getting drafted. This was long before there was a lottery. You just got yanked, out of the blue. "What do you need?" I said. He told me, "Nothing." He was going to try to fail the physical. He had some ideas about it. Then he told me about a job he had that he couldn't do now. It was shutting some summer house down. He had told the lady whose house it was that he couldn't do it, but he'd send someone. He asked me if I wanted to take it. It sounded good to me. Ana had already left for college in Amherst. I was getting ready to go to New York and write poems, which is how I thought one did it—just go off and write. I liked the idea of a few more dollars before I took off. "Can you give me twenty for it?" Santos asked. "For the job?" I looked into his face, and he wasn't kidding. I had never seen anybody our age that sad before. I gave him two tens. I never saw him again.

It was a big yellow house pretty far down the East End on the side of Commercial Street opposite the water. The woman's name was Miss de Beers, but I knew who she was just from town talk. She was Moses Hammond's wife, and he did not summer in Provincetown with her. Hammond, as the fishermen liked to say, was richer than God. He was the scion of Walter Hammond, who built superior marine engines and parlayed his success with them into a large marine supply corporation. Several of the high-line boats in our fleet ran Hammond power plants.

Miss de Beers was a slender woman with light eyes and that shade of hair that can't decide between blonde and silver. She was not young—I couldn't guess her age, but she had one of those faces where you could see the waning prettiness of the younger person shining though the small lines at the corners of her eyes and mouth. She was sunbaked, and her arms and hands were darkly freckled. She looked me over pretty hard. "What is your name in Portuguese," she said. I told her and pronounced it for her.

She sighed. "That will never do," she said. "You will have to be François, dear boy."

"Charles Dickens," I said.

"Yes?" she said.

"*Great Expectations*. Miss Havisham. The 'dear boy'."

She put her hands on her hips. "You've got the job," she said. "You can stop showing off now."

It was an easy job, just packing the house and mulching the plants. Winterizing. A lot of things were going to stay, but she wanted them covered. A load of loam was coming from Wellfleet, and I had to wheelbarrow it and spread it around the backyard. It was the end of the season, but people were still coming and going, having lunches or drinks on the porch. Miss de Beers liked to tell her friends I was her Portuguese boy, and she'd make a big deal about introducing me, like it was a funny thing to do. If I was sweating, she would call me over. "Take your shirt off and drink this, dear boy," she'd say, and she'd give me a glass of ice water or some kind of Kool-Aid. "Put your hat on too," she would tell me. Her tone was bossy when *she* was showing off—but then she was the boss.

She was yet another artist, though she told me in a confidential tone that she was only a student. I had to organize her studio, stack canvasses against the wall, and cover them with plastic tarps. She painted a lot of nudes, all kinds—boys, girls, men, women. They were brightly colored and blocky—not abstract as far as I knew, but not realistic either. One of them actually looked very much like Renata. Her naked body stretched a bit out of proportion, long and angled. She was standing with her hands behind her back and looking upward at something. It was the last thing I put away.

I reached New York with a duffle bag of clothes, some cash, Miss de Beers's check for three hundred dollars (an enormous sum in those days), and a 1936 Underwood Portable typewriter that my mother's former husband, Manny (who was not my father), had bought for me from a going-out-of-business sale at a little sandwich shop that had opened too far into the West End to survive. I had been in the tenth grade when he bought it. I had told him I was going to be a writer and I wanted to take typing in school, which I did and got a D. He told my mother it had cost five dollars but I knew it had cost ten because of the little white tag under the case. He hadn't wanted to sound like he'd spent too much money on it. They would have fought about it. It turned out to be an important typewriter.

I found a place right away, a rooming house way over on the West Side on Thirtieth Street. There were four other people living on the top floor then, and they were musicians more or less and were putting a band together. We were all friends immediately. The building was old, dark brick and mortar with iron fire escapes and a long staircase with landings all the way up to the fourth floor. The street was lined with similar buildings, and on the corner down on Eighth Avenue there was a small grocery store and deli that sold just about anything a person could want.

I was not in a hurry to get a job, so once I got settled, I went to cash my check from Miss de Beers at the nearest bank. The teller told me that I would have to go to her own bank uptown, the one printed on the check. When I got there the teller refused to cash it. She pointed out the signature on the check and then the name printed in the top left-hand corner. Nina de Beers and Mrs. Moses Hammond.

I found her building easily up on East 78th Street, but there was a doorman and every time I told him who I was and why I was there he would tell me Mrs. Hammond was not at home. This went on for a while until I told him that I worked on Mrs. Hammond's property in Provincetown and that I knew some town kids who were going to break into the house.

That got Miss de Beers's attention, but she still ran me around for a while, having me come up to her rather grand apartment a number of times before she finally just gave me cash. On that particular visit, two things of significance happened. She offered me a job, and Renata was there, sitting on a long white couch, her bare feet up on a very modern-looking glass coffee table, smoking a cigarette.

They were lovers of course; even I could tell that, and Moses Hammond was in Southeast Asia working on shipping and husbanding deals that were already in bids because of the growing war in Vietnam. The women were working on a plan of their own. Miss de Beers had bought an old bank building downtown and was turning the ground floor into a gallery. The first show was to be Renata's box art. She was working on new pieces. My job was going to be messenger, gopher, and general worker around the gallery and apartment. Renata and Nina seemed different in one another's company. When I was with one or the other by themselves their personalities changed—in Renata's case she returned to someone very much like the Renata I knew in Provincetown. With Nina she affected an edginess and kept a distance, which is to say she became more like Nina. I hadn't been around for more than a couple of weeks when Renata showed up at the apartment with a small box of what turned out to be morphine suppositories. Nina was eager for them and made it clear that I was going to do one too. I could tell that she and Renata had talked about this, but I cannot imagine the conversation. Renata knew that I was no stranger to experimentation. I think Nina simply wanted to make me complicit, a kind of insurance against I had no idea what, but there we were in a living room on the Upper East Side with our pants down applying the gizmos to one another. The effect was long and euphoric. I found that this sort of thing was not a singular occurrence.

It was during this time that a whole new light began to shine on Renata, Moses Hammond, and Nina de Beers. I gathered some of this information from just being around the two women, but another source of the narrative was a woman named Elaine, a designer who was working on the gallery conversion and who had a history of working with Nina. Only three of my notebooks survived that time in New York, and I searched them out of my attic crawlspace after I began reading Renata's manuscript. They contain the embarrassing entries and musings of a young man trying to be a poet, and they are woefully incomplete—not in any sense diaries—but I did write dialogues, hasty notes, and conversations in them, and once I started going through them, I was happy to see how often Elaine showed up on the pages. Her last name does not appear anywhere. I had described her as "older, about 40 with glasses and dark sweaters. Very smart. Cool." Not a brilliant description, but reading the words conjured her in my memory in a pleasing way and helped to bring her back to life for me. Some of the information that I transcribe here was spread out in disparate conversations and entries. I have pulled some of these together for the sake of readability.

Elaine and I would sit around and talk a lot. She liked to grouse about the gallery project, but she was always half serious about it. The grumbling was like a sport for her. She could be funny and acerbic at the same time. I always brought her black coffee in a cardboard cup when I delivered posts and papers to her down at the building where she was creating the gallery. We both seemed to have time to waste on our jobs, although Elaine was a serious professional and I saw this by watching her. She knew more about how the gallery was coming along than Nina and Renata did. And she knew a lot about Nina and Renata, period.

She told me how Nina, when Elaine started working on the project, had told her she had gone to Bryn Mawr and studied literature there. She told her about life there and shouting to Athena and putting on musicals and so forth. Lots of detail. But when Elaine mentioned this to Renata in passing, Renata flipped. "She told you that? She told you that? That was me. *I* went to Bryn Mawr! Jesus Christ." Elaine was laughing telling me this. She imitated Renata yelling about it.

"So, who was right?" I asked.

"Oh God, probably neither one of them, but if I had to, I'd bet Renata. I know she has an M.A. from someplace. But Nina just appropriates things. All that de Beers stuff, you know." Elaine told me that Nina's name was Ruth something or other, and she was born in West Virginia and never went to college at all. Moses met her when he was down there looking at some business for his father. "Maybe it was one of those Pygmalion things," Elaine said. "And evidently Moses just needed a wife."

It was from Elaine that I learned Moses Hammond once had designs on Renata, who worked and traveled with him translating documents and brokering marine supplies. According to Elaine, Moses, with his empire, had no real need for Renata—

he could have found a translator anywhere, though her quick expertise in the marine supply business had surely been an asset. But Elaine said he had hired her with the idea of taking her as young lover, which of course did not work out, and she and Nina somehow fell for each other. Moses and Nina were hardly ever in the same place at the same time, so the women were always in one another's company, and all of this seemed to mean nothing to Hammond anyway. But sometime in the previous spring something had happened involving hard drugs. It could have been pharmaceuticals, like the morphine—Elaine either didn't specify or I didn't write it down—and the consequence of it was that both were "persons of interest" concerning some fairly serious charges (though it is hard to imagine how that would have come about). Moses somehow made the incident go away, but he wanted to erase the whole episode. A not unreasonable surmise here is that he feared that legal difficulties might somehow become attached to his name and the business, especially given his working closely with the government. One might also speculate that Moses used some sort of contractual lever on Renata, because he banished her from Nina's life. Renata did not seem like someone who would go away easily, but Elaine was very clear about how powerful Hammond was. So now with Renata and Nina back together in the city, Elaine was anxious about the whole gallery business. She saw it as a recipe for disaster. Moses was supposedly in the dark about all this. He was out of the country doing business at very high levels. He was also traveling or living with a woman whom Miss de Beers would only call Mrs. Simpson, which went right over my head until Renata told me what it implied: "It makes Moses a sort of king, you see," she said. "An abdicated king."

Hammond at this time, regardless of his affairs of the flesh, was negotiating contracts for shipping and marine husbandry (a term Nina made much of when she lapsed into tirades about him) in preparation for the developing war.

The war was an interesting matter for Nina and Renata. When I was with them at the apartment, the atmosphere would sometimes feel like a knife fight, with each of them committed to not cutting the other. The rooms would grow very cold, but you could sense an immeasurable conflagration smoldering underneath. Renata was already involved in antiwar protests and moved in radical circles. Nina, I think, would sometimes show some distaste for what was happening to the country—in the streets of New York at least, but she never openly condemned it. It was an odd kind of dodgeball game, but Renata told me once, that despite everything, Nina would always be glued to Moses. It never mattered what things might look like. The war was more money for Hammond Marine. Enormous sums. And Nina understood this.

The drugs were another matter. Renata and I had smoked dope together in Provincetown of course, and I would have guessed that Renata was the one who turned Nina on to the morphine. Well, maybe this was true or maybe not, but Nina was the one who always pushed for it. She always made sure that Renata kept a supply. I could see that Nina was not about to look for sources or commit herself to buying dope on her own. She greatly depended on Renata for this. It was another one of those oscillations, part of a force field they shared. Through it all, you could see that there persisted some unidentifiable feeling, some kinetic attraction between them. It was exhausting sometimes just to sit in the same room with them.

And then there was the business. Nina was going to open La Gallerie Nina in the old bank building. Renata's work would be the opening exhibit. Elaine, on one occasion, told me that Renata could never have her own exclusive show in any other gallery, that she just didn't have that kind of platform yet. And Nina was pouring money into getting the building into shape, and she was talking up Renata in helpful circles. So they each had a stake in one another. Elaine voiced her wariness or uncertainty about the venture, but I assume she was getting paid very well for her services. Part of my job with Nina—who was always Miss de Beers to me—was running messages. There was always a great deal of paper going back and forth between the apartment, where she kept her office—and the gallery. I also ran documents to other buildings around the city. Miss de Beers had even bought me a suit to wear and a leather briefcase to carry when I went to certain companies, banks, law offices, and other businesses that were ostentatious in their displays of wealth and importance.

Other parts of my job consisted in doing anything she wanted me to do. Sometimes she would just have me sit around and listen to her talk. Sometimes she'd sketch me or paint me, and this usually segued into other activities. She talked a lot about Moses, and she sent me down to Renata's studio almost daily on some errand or another. She continually quizzed me about her. Does she really go there? What is she doing? Is she working on the pieces? You wouldn't believe the expense, just for artwork, plywood, nails, tools. The paint alone . . ."

Renata knew what Nina was up to. She laughed about it. She also warned me, more than once. Don't think you know more than she does, *Coitado*. She is an omnivore. Don't think you are going to come out ahead. Be careful around her."

I said, "Are you careful?"

Renata lit a cigarette and blew out a funnel of smoke before she answered. "Probably not," she said.

I don't think it was so much that Nina was predatory—or perhaps she was, but from my vantage she seemed more like proprietary. It was a natural force in her. It was the only evidence of calm or stillness about her. There was even an odd grace to it. She simply and profoundly understood that everything and everybody in her ambit was her very own possession. She saw herself as taking good care of all that belonged to her. She believed herself to be generous and progressive. "Pretty much anything you could possibly think or say about her would be true," Renata said to me one day. "She's bought you nice clothes, she pays you pretty well for running all over town for her. She paints you nude. Not so badly, really. But be wary about the sex, *Coitado*. Don't try to figure out what it means."

Of course Renata would know about that. It was part of this new world, and I certainly hadn't figured out what it meant yet.

"I don't think too much about it," I remember telling her. It was not unpleasant. "It's like a subway train carrying me off into a really strange new land."

"Of course," said Renata. "Far Rockaway."

It just came out of me then, easy as breath. "It's you I'm devoted to, Renata," I said. "You're the one I love."

She looked at me. Her dark eyes narrowed in the smallest degree. "I know," she said.

When Renata was with you, she accelerated you. There was something adrenal about her presence. I could see that is what happened with Nina. When Nina was by herself, she was a woman who loved art, but only sometimes. She leaned hard against the fences of that world, but never with her full weight. She was an attractive, cultured middle-aged woman who painted nudes and then sometimes tutored them on how to please her. You inferred that she lived with the knowledge that in her life she had missed something very important. Painting, collecting, and now building a gallery were things that she did, but they were not her life. They were more like transient dance partners in a carnival ballroom. But when Renata was with her, Nina might have felt like she was finally exercising her soul. You could tell by how she held herself, how she talked. She must have seen a light somewhere, some dubious star she was finally flying toward. I think I knew that feeling. Nina wanted to be Renata. So did I.

When I was down at the studio with Renata we spent a lot of time just telling stories and laughing. I was happy with how much she seemed to like my hanging around. My notebooks here are messy, but I clearly spent more time writing things down in them, things she told me, subjects she talked about. If the notes I took during this narrow band in the spectrum of her life have any bearing at all on the woman who would write the poems, perhaps they might offer some small insight into her character. She was generous and without boundaries. I felt liked by her in a way that I had not felt liked before. That is, she seemed to take an interest in what I was doing and where I thought I was going. She never talked down to me, but she seemed to enjoy scolding me along with offering advice. There was always an edge of humor in such moments, as though she were entertaining both of us.

Against one wall of her studio there were two mismatched bookcases, both painted a glossy yellow and filled with all sorts of volumes, ratty paperbacks, hardcovers, textbooks, art books. "Everything you need," Renata said when she saw me staring at them. Then she paused a beat and corrected herself. "I mean you in particular need everything you see here." She randomly pulled out six books with quick movements of her hand. "So start," she said. In my notebook I wrote down those first authors. Rimbaud, Dickinson, Baldwin, Jung, Woolf, and Frank O'Hara.

We talked a lot about Provincetown during those times but not in any discursive way. We somehow could feed on each other, finding so many crazy things about the place and talking about predicaments we had found ourselves in. And there were many characters, townies and summer people. For instance, we both knew Theodora, a marvelous drag queen who bragged outrageously about all the sex she was having with straight guys, and how they never knew for a moment she wasn't a girl. Renata and I would riff on stories about her, making up all sorts of what-if scenarios. Renata could roll you up on the floor and have you in tears laughing. "I like your head, man," she'd say. And then I'd say, "I like your head, man." This somehow became an exchange that would crack us up. There didn't seem any reason for it.

But she could brood, too. She'd go through spells that she called *tormentas*. She could disappear from the studio and from Nina's for days. If Nina asked her where she went, Renata's face would fight with itself for a few seconds, but she would say nothing. Sometimes at the studio she would sit on the couch, smoking in silence, just looking out the windows, while I read, wrote in a notebook, or neatened up the piles of wood and salvage in the workshop opposite the living space. This was her melancholy time, a bearing I had never witnessed back in Provincetown when she seemed always in a social mode—biking, visiting, cruising, reveling. It was during one of these gloomy spells when she told me that sinking into yourself like this was important for certain kinds of people. That if you found that you were one of those souls, then it was part of something you had to do, that you had to understand the dark part of yourself. She said it comes after you when you try to move forward on something, anything. You had to learn its ways and subterfuges. When you don't, it gets exactly what it wants.

"What does your dark part want?" I said.

"Same thing as yours, *Coitado*. It wants you to fail. The truth is that it really wants you dead."

When her storms would pass, as they always did, I helped around the studio and helped her in her salvaging forays around the city. We built a kind of dolly to haul stuff with—broken dressers and trunks, boxes of all kinds, planks. Her studio was located on the fourth floor of her building, and you could tell it had been a loft of some kind, possibly a sail loft or perhaps something to do with textiles (this speculation is written in my notebook—I doubt I had any real clue about what it was). An alley ran along the back of the building, and in the rear of the studio a raised section of flooring abutted an old double door, which still opened onto the alley, four floors up, and still had its wooden boom with a block and tackle, which we rerigged with strong sisal rope. This let us haul material up to the floor, obviating the likely impossible task of getting all of our salvage up the staircases.

The loft itself was a single space whose only small dividing wall enclosed the toilet. Even the bath was out in the open, near the part of the wall that was the kitchen, where Renata had rigged up a showerhead for the tub, on the end of a red rubber enema hose. Along with the yellow bookcases there was a cast-iron sink, a narrow gas stove and refrigerator, a big mattress on the floor, a couch and some chairs, and in the far north end her workshop proper—benches, tables, tools, boards, shelves of paint. On good days the space was suffused with a dusty light coming through three tall windows on the eastern wall. It was a place Renata could work in but could live in as well, and I knew that she did not always stay with Nina.

City Renata was different from Provincetown Renata. The over-alls and work shirts never left her studio. She dressed in black col-

lared shirts and tight pants, usually also black, and with silver ear-
rings and leather boots. She could dazzle. Her hair was dark and
thicker now, and her skin was like cream, but with the touch of
café com leite that might have seemed like a Provincetown suntan
that had not yet left her. She looked very much Portuguese, and to
my mind she displayed those bloodlines with edge and glamour.
She was unlike the girls and women I knew in the West End. She
cast a complicated but very palpable energy around herself. Not
energy like vigor, though she was vigorous, but something that
drew you in so you could feel yourself tumbling into her light,
despite what she said about her shadows. But as you fell into her
gravity you felt an alternate pull, too. She vibrated, and you didn't
want to get in her way or stall her momentum. You were often
pinned at a small distance from her center. What her center was,
you couldn't guess. And her vigor, when it did come into play,
resembled passion.

It was about this time I learned how exercised she had become
over the war and its progression into our daily lives, even as we
lived in the relative privilege of our towering cities and our igno-
rance—all this was something I should have known more about.
The Cold War was like a fog around us in those days, and every-
one in the city had some opinion about the bombs and missiles.
People sang about them in protest in Washington Square, and
there were shelter signs plastered up and down the platforms on
the subway lines. You couldn't escape the thought that you might
be incinerated at any moment. It was just something you learned
to live with in your fantasies. I liked to see myself hanging a leg
over the window in my room, drinking a beer and watching for
the blast, the kind of delusion you can conjure when nothing is
at stake for you. Vietnam intruded on this malaise in sharp and
pointed ways. Vietnam, we were learning, was in your face and
nasty. It was mean-spirited and said something more immediate

and unnerving about the venal men in charge of our country. In this regard Renata was very much the leftist American. Renata came at things from many directions, as unpredictable as the wind. She attended protests, which were now showing up around the city in various sizes and differing intensities, but she also studied events from diverse angles, and could quote history and facts that I did not think were available from our radios and newspapers. For instance, she knew a great deal about Moses Hammond's interest in the wars—she called them imperial wars or colonial wars—and how Hammond Marine was investing great sums into the MSTS Charters—that is, the Military Sea Transportation Service. The United States needed 720,000 tons of privately owned shipping (about sixty or seventy ships) to transport supplies and equipment to Vietnam. Hammond was also brokering the husbanding services, which, she said, were the cleaning, maintenance, docking, and various other functions, invisible or overlooked, without which fleets of heavy ships would cease to operate and rust in desolation on their moorings. She said Hammond was exploring ways to not only profit from his Vietnam involvement but also to capitalize on Portugal's wars in Africa with his shipping and husbanding infrastructure. I had never heard about Portugal fighting in Africa.

Renata could hold complicated matters in her fist and then parse them for you, reducing them to simplicity, like an adept morphologist diagramming a sentence. It is likely that it was about this time or over these issues that Renata broke off professionally from Hammond, not disregarding the fact that there surely would have been some cause and effect touching upon Nina. Renata schooled me on the inside stories of war: profit for the rich. She expressed concern about me and the draft. She turned me on to Karl Marx and his analysis of capital. She gave me copies of the *Guardian*, the *Nation*, the *Daily Worker*.

The hammer fell upon all this, of course. It was inevitable. The war in Vietnam was truly ramping up and so was the resistance, and the draft board had sent someone to my mother's house in Provincetown looking for me. Renata and Nina de Beers were now locked in some sort of drama that I did not completely understand yet. My last surviving notebook becomes spotty right here. I was hanging out now with the band on the top floor, and though I couldn't play an instrument, I was writing lyrics for their songs. We lived in four rooms, an arrangement that effectively turned the whole floor into one odd apartment. There was a single large bathroom and a shower on the hallway, and a payphone on the wall near my door. My room had the one aged kitchenette on the floor, and everybody used it. The leader of the band was Ronnie, a guitarist and owner of a red Triumph 650 motorcycle. Even when he was indoors and standing still, his long hair remained blown back on his head as though he were roaring at 100 miles per hour. His girlfriend, Rainey, was long and willowy with jet black hair that flowed down below her shoulders. She fronted the band when Ronnie wasn't singing, and danced with a tambourine when he was. A wild man named Lloyd played the drums, and his brother Dexter, who looked less wild, played the bass. Lloyd had just bought an old Volkswagen Microbus, and he had read *On the Road* and fell in love with Neal Cassady, whose maniac driving habits he practiced. Getting around seemed worth your life, but the van rocked and rolled with all the equipment tied down in the back and three of us jammed on the bench seat in front. Ronnie and Rainey always roared in on the Triumph. The idea was to get some songs down, get some money, and go to San Francisco. The band had started playing in downtown cellars, little places near the docks, and over in New Jersey. Real joints. I got to go on most of the gigs because they were in the far late hours when

Nina only rarely summoned me to her apartment. Ronnie had called the band Top Floor, but no one was too high on that, and after we all had a meeting I prevailed, and the band became Far Rockaway.

It was just about this time when Renata asked me to go cruising pawn shops with her to see if she could pick up a typewriter. She said she was starting to write a play. She said you had to have a typewriter for a play. It was the only way you could get it right. The play was going to be about a Portuguese fisherman running a small dragger in Provincetown and his young daughter, whom he had taken out of school to crew for him. "What happens to them?" I asked.

"I don't know," she said. "You're not supposed to know, you're supposed to find out when you write it. That's how it works. If you already knew, what would be the point?"

I remember that I didn't have an answer for her, or even another question. Finally, I told her that I had a machine and we could share it. At first she resisted, but in the end she liked the story of how my mother's husband Manny had bought it for me, and she thought for a while. "That's important." She said. "That man. That's a very important thing for you." No explanation. But we had a deal. It worked out perfectly. There was so much commotion, smoking, hanging out, and drifting from room to room at the house that I needed a quiet place to read and write, so I moved the Underwood to the studio where we put it on a small square table that Renata had painted fire engine red, and she used the machine for her play when I wasn't around. And I wrote poems and lyrics on it when *she* wasn't around. I was happy with the arrangement and with the band, and it took me a while to notice how often Renata wasn't home, and when I did notice, I didn't think about it much. The Microbus, though I didn't think about it much either, plays a small part in these accounts.

The longest and most detailed notebook entry I possess was made shortly after November 9, 1965. It was Thursday, late afternoon, and I had taken the subway downtown and walked to Renata's loft carrying a sheaf of papers in my leather briefcase. I was fairly certain that none of the documents I carried from Miss de Beers were very important, but I knew that Nina would want a report from me. She was always very nervous when Renata didn't come around, and she hadn't been uptown in several days.

Renata had been working when I arrived. I loved the workshop end of her loft—boards and power saws, and big strips of paper on the wall with drawings on them, boxes and sketches, people and lines in every angle and color. There were stacks of cans and buckets; the whole place smelled like linseed oil and paint and cut wood, and then the smell of her, Renata herself: the underarms of her shirt and the cigarette smoke on her breath lifted a dizzying fume into the air around her, complicated and sexy.

She opened two beers and we sat on the couch and talked briefly about the documents I had brought. Contracts, Renata told me, and shook her head. I could tell she was tense or distracted. Jittery. She moved the valise aside with her foot. Dusk had come on, and the tall windows were dark and sequestering. The little radio on top of the refrigerator was turned down low, and a woman was singing something from an opera, sad and beautiful. I asked Renata what it was. She said, "Puccini," and then the radio died and all the lights went out.

At first Renata thought it was the fuse box. The sun had set, and it was already pretty dark in the loft. She flicked her lighter and started to walk over to the corner wall, but I looked out the window and said, "It's everything. Everything is out."

She rifled through some drawers and found some candles

and lit them and we talked for a while in low tones standing at the windows. The whole city was dark, and a huge moon was just rising over the buildings toward the east. It was eerie. There were sirens and voices down in the street. Shouts. I don't know how long we stood there, but finally I remember saying, "Missiles. Maybe it's finally the missiles." I thought maybe we should run down to the subway where the orange and black shelter signs hung gloomily on the walls among advertisements for rye bread and toothpaste, though I don't think anyone believed that the subway tunnels would keep us from being vaporized. Renata thought for a bit. "No, I don't think so. They'd be here, the missiles What does it take? Thirty minutes, I think they say." She was agitated though. "Maybe it's sabotage. Like it has something to do with that guy who set himself on fire this morning." I hadn't heard about this. She told me about him, a Catholic Worker, who burned himself in front of the United Nations building to protest the war. She said he was still alive, but no one expected him to live. She talked about another man, this one a Quaker, who had immolated himself a few days earlier in front of the Pentagon. And of course Buddhist monks in Saigon serially set themselves afire in the streets, as photographs and film clips too often reminded us. It was plausible. All the deaths stirring up emotions. Now the people rising up, attacking the electric grid.

"Something's not right," Renata said.

The atmosphere in the big room had changed now, nerves were firing. *Renata's* nerves were firing. I had seen her like this before, but never to this degree. She might have been taking Dexedrine that day, but whatever the case, the scene was frightening. We crept down the darkened flights of stairs to the sidewalk, where we found some men listening to a big portable radio. They had found a station from Illinois, scratchy voices talking over the fact that they knew almost nothing. "It's the whole East Coast," one of the men said. "It's the fucking Russians," said another. We made our way back to the top floor and climbed through the trapdoor that led to the roof. The city was dark, the moon was shining, and wan tiny lights flickered and glowed in windows here and there. Candles or battery lanterns. You could hear some cars moving in the distance. The wind was coming off the river, cold. Renata was shivering. We stood there for a while, and if we said anything then I did not make any make notes about it. It was chilly, and we didn't know anything. We climbed down and went back to the studio where the candles still trembled, bouncing in some drafty volume of air that only their flames could sense.

I am sure it must have been that compounding darkness, the situation vast but unknown, the atmosphere of war and agitation and the constant but muted specter of complete annihilation that was always there—and how the room itself seemed to compress our emotions—for Renata began talking, chain smoking, leaning toward me, going on, following threads of thought. "This country is fucked," she said. "I know about these things. We are on the edge of something. This all could be the government, *Coitado*. Maybe they are suppressing the grid to show an iron fist. They don't like people in the streets demonstrating, resisting. It will get worse, you'll see. Fascists love a foreign war. Christ, in the *New York Times* of America last week. Salazar."

"Wait, I said, what's Salazar?"

She stabbed her cigarette out and glared at me for a moment. It was a rebuke. "Jesus, *Coitado*, not what. Who. A fascist dictator. Portuguese. The *Times* had his picture in the paper last week, a story about how wonderful he is. You didn't see it? He was posed like a fucking priest." She always kept after me to stay current with the news. "You want to be cannon fodder?" she'd say. "You have to keep your head out of your ass, *Coitado.*" I'd heard this kind of thing from her before, but always with an even tone, like she was giving me advice. Now even the weak light of the candles showed it on her face—she was smoldering.

I didn't say anything, but the talking definitely pivoted here. It would be the first time she ever talked with me in this particular register. There was something of an equality to it as though I were her peer, for she started quietly telling about her father. He worked in Lisbon before the war, and he was outspoken against Hitler and Mussolini, which, she said, was dangerous at the time because António Salazar was forming his own fascist government in Portugal. Her father, though, was a popular journalist and highly placed, and he believed he had latitude in his editorial pieces. Perhaps he did, but as Renata told it, he crossed some vital border. There was a dinner party at the Ferreira home one night—not unusual—but she thought she remembered the very night it happened, for her mother would speak about it later. Renata had been put to bed upstairs, and the talk and the laughter kept her awake into the night. Evidently her father had written a piece that was a savage satire attacking Salazar's personal character. It was never intended to be published. He had written it for the entertainment of his friends, and he read it to them that night. He was arrested several days later. Renata spoke now seriously and matter-of-factly, and this seemed worse than anger or passion. There was something brutal about it, and for a time the sequester of the studio felt like a crevasse in a black field of ice. I would ascribe that now to our abraded nerves during that inexplicable darkness, but Renata was like a glove turned inside out, and I could see how she labored at her tale.

Her father had been betrayed, of course, by someone who had sat in his home and broken bread at his table. There had been an attempt on the dictator's life. Unions and students rallied against the fascist government. This was the analogy to our own situation that she was making for me, but New York was hardly Lisbon, and everything seemed far off and improbable. Then she spoke of Tarrafal. This I learned was a prison camp, a concentration camp, as she described it, modeled on the grim German camps that the Salazar government had studied, and it was located in the Cape Verde Islands, off Africa. Her father had been an intransigent man, and whatever trouble he had caused, he exacerbated it, and provoked the wrong people. He was sent to Tarrafal and died there in a manner of punishment whereby men were placed in a small box in the sun and baked to death. The guards, not without a dark sense of humor, called it the refrigerator. Partisans called it the camp of the slow death.

I was uneasy and did not comprehend my part in this conversation, if that is what it was. In any case I said little. I was seeing something of her inner ranges, and I was working hard to reconcile them to the Renata I thought I knew. I was out of my depth then, and some of the judgments I offer come from me, now, decades later as I revisit the tatter of information that remains of these events, though it's impossible to know the stories behind Renata's account. I remember feeling thrown by all this, trying to keep up with this new part of her and this strange history about which I had known nothing. And as with so much of Renata's essence, there would be inaccuracies in her history, and a vigorous contradiction to the version of her father's death and her escape to America. But that would come later from an unlikely source.

Renata went on, smoking, jittering. She shook her head, fanned smoke away from her face. There was the feeling of air having been let out of the room, and Renata might have regretted going off into her rant. There was a silence I didn't know how to break, but finally she leaned in and said, "I'm talking too much about Portugal, but, you know, there's a lot of shit in the world, man. Look, you're a Portuguese kid from the West End of Provincetown, all those old folks still speaking Portuguese, planting their kale gardens, salting cod. I mean, it's beautiful, really. It's like those complicated nautilus creatures. They carried their homes on their backs. They created a new Portugal out of the old one. It's like art. They made up a new country for themselves, but I have to tell you there is a kind of indifference about it. Nothing matters except what happens right there. No ideas, no politics. You know Ana's grandmother had high blood pressure, and Doctor Hiebert gave her some pills and put her on a diet. She was having none of that diet business, though. She said that she didn't come to this country to be hungry. She said, 'When I die, I'm going to die with my belly full.' That was her truth, and it was a beautiful truth. It was pure. There's a beauty to all those people and that town. But that beauty can be insular too. You can get stuck in the picture. You get that, I know. You left that place. I'd say you *fled* it."

"I did flee it," I said.

"Yeah, sure," she said. "Except you can't. You'll see." She paused and took a breath. "You'll carry it with you in your blood."

I saw the look on her face. "Is that talking about *you*, now?" I said.

She didn't answer. She crushed her cigarette and walked to the windows. The moon. The darkness and shadows so weird on the rooftops and water towers.

"And here *you* are, *Coitado*. Yeah, there's a lot of shit going on in the world. There's a lot going on right here. You've got to be ready. The worst thing you can do when the shit hits the fan is keep your head down." She lit another cigarette with the stub of the old one, sighed, got up, paced. "I'm in a mood, *Coitado*. I don't like the way I sound right now."

"So what's the best thing to do, then? I said.

"What?"

"When all that shit hits the fan. What's the best thing to do?"

She hung her head for a moment. A look of melancholy came over her face, but it was like the shadow of a bird flitting past. It vanished with whatever thought that was behind it. She looked at me. "Be the fan," she said.

We stood then in the windows and didn't talk for a while. I don't know how long. Not much had changed. The moon was higher now, whiter, and the light seemed to blow down from it like salt. Sometimes there was a siren. Suddenly Renata spun away from the glass. "Jesus Christ," she said, "I wish I knew what the hell was going on."

My head was spinning. I said something just to not be silent. "No bombs, no missiles."

We were both exhausted. Renata said, "Fuck all this. I'm getting off."

"Me too, then," I said.

She hesitated a moment, then said, "All right." She walked across the room and came back with her works and a little paper packet. The notebook entry ends with two fragments and two complete sentences:

Nodding on the mattress. Bliss and dreaming.

We leaned together and our bodies pressed.

We were so warm.

I didn't make notes for a long time after the Great Blackout, as it was called, but I remember spending time with the band, which was not yet making any money, but they gave a good show when they could get gigs, which was harder when the winter came. I think our songs sounded okay. I was still running around for Nina, and hanging out at Renata's where I wrote a lot, as she came and went pretty freely and I noticed that the work on the boxes had slowed down. She wasn't doing much. Renata was using all through this time, and doing Dexedrine off and on, but I don't think she had a habit. Nina was using too, still the morphine, and I am pretty sure I saw her sick more than once, and later she and Renata had a row about Renata abandoning her. I think this meant not keeping the supply going as much as Nina would have liked, but Nina also would not let go of the idea that Renata was seeing someone else.

Renata was indeed seeing someone else. She told me so and told me that Nina was not in any shape to hear that yet. And I could tell that her work in the studio had fallen off, and I believed she was spending time at the Underwood, and spending time with her new lover. And I was loyal to Renata and falsely assured Nina that all was well, and I had seen no one, nor any evidence of another woman. This last part was actually the truth. There was never a trace of anyone visiting her studio other than myself.

If the artwork had fallen behind, that was simply one worry. Another problem was the gallery. Nina had wanted to open in spring, not so far off by this time, and there were problems with the building. I had figured this out from all the dispatches, bids, blueprints, invoices, bills, checks, contracts, and paper I had been carting around town. Nina was pouring more money into the renovations.

I got down to the old bank early on a Monday morning. It might have been March. In my notebook there is nothing to calibrate the time with, no notation of foliage or rain or what clothing I wore. Still not dating the entries, I had put Monday down because the Met would be open free all day. I had an envelope for Elaine.

There was work of some kind being done to one of the walls

on the second floor, where I found Elaine sitting at a table made
of two sawhorses and a narrow sheet of plywood. The surface
was neatly organized into a desk, with the sort of expensive trap-
pings you might find in a fancy office—lots of leather and brass,
a crystal ashtray and a lavish gooseneck lamp. Papers and fold-
ers were tidily stacked, and I knew this came from Elaine's sense
of humor because there was chaos all around her—crumpled
concrete, stacks of rebar, rubble, lumber, machines that were be-
yond my experience to name. She had made an art piece in the
middle of it. I set down the paper cup of coffee I always brought
her. She did not look like she was in a good mood. When she
opened the envelope nothing in her face changed, but she said
the word "Christ."

She looked at me and said, "I should have seen this coming.
I fucking *saw* it coming and ignored it because I was worrying
about those two lunatics you work for. I saw it for the last couple
of months. I don't know how this all got to him, but you can tell
Nina it wasn't me who blew the whistle." It turned out that Nina
somehow had been using huge amounts money from Moses's
holdings and Moses found out about it. He found out about the
whole plan with Renata, the show, that one of the leases for a
"warehouse" was actually Renata's studio, everything. I can see
now that Renata was probably at the snapping point. It's a good
bet that he suspected the dope again. He knew his wife after all.
"Look," Elaine said, "it's déjà vu. He's coming into town tomor-
row. It's another fucking disaster. Actually, it's the same disaster
all over again except for this." She indicated the building with a
sweeping gesture of her hand, still holding the letter. "I wanted
this building too much. I could transform it. It would be beauti-
ful." She lit a cigarette and passed it to me, lit one for herself,
and picked up the coffee. She told me she had let too much
slide, had seen the odd way money was being moved around.

She told me again how she wanted the building. "That was the bottom line for me. This is really not good."

We talked more for a while. We rehashed some things. "You know Moses really hated Renata," she said. "When all that shit came down last year, he told me that nothing about her was real. He did some checking about her. All that about fleeing the country because the fascists killed her father. *Her father was one of them.* He was right there, and he helped put that prison camp together down in the Canary Islands or wherever. Moses is not someone to fuck with. He wanted to do dirt to Renata for sure, but I believed him. He is a guy who gets things right." I didn't know what to say about that. Today I don't see how it made much difference what she said. Things go like that. But Hammond did plant doubt about other things Renata said about herself. I don't know how much that matters. So she was inventing selves. So what? But back then, all of that really shook me up. I remember being very confused. Hurt even, in some childish way. We talked a little more after that, I don't remember about what. As I left Elaine said, "Get out quick, Frankie."

It all went quick.

I didn't go back to Nina's for a couple of days. I hung out at Renata's studio hoping she would show up, but she didn't, and so I went back to the rooming house and crashed. It was about three in the morning when Nina called the payphone in the hall. I had been asleep before answering, but Lloyd was up with his door open. He stepped out into the hall. I covered the receiver with the palm of my hand. "Can I take the van?" I said. Lloyd nodded and said, "What?"

"Some bad shit," I said.

"Let's go then," he said. "I'll drive."

Lloyd never asked a thing. I just told him where to go, and we balled uptown with the little engine whining and Lloyd driving like we were on fire. You could smell hot oil from the pistons. I told Lloyd what Nina had said to me on the phone. Renata had passed out. She was unconscious. She had to go to an emergency room. Lloyd asked why Nina didn't call an ambulance, but, really, we already had a good idea why.

We got there in minutes and pulled right up to front of the building. There was no one at the door, but it had been left unlocked. We didn't wait for the elevator; we ran up the stairs. When we entered the apartment, I knew immediately that the florid portly man in a white dress shirt with the sleeves rolled up was Moses Hammond. "What the hell is this?" he said to Nina as we walked in. He tried to keep a tone of disgust in his voice, but I was not about to be afraid of him, and Lloyd took a step toward him like someone who would kill without provocation, which could have been true.

Moses paced and raged, but I could tell he was the one who was terrified. Nina was silent, standing away from him. Her own face was pale, almost green in the strange light of the foyer. Her mouth was compressed into a narrow line that made her cheeks look swollen. Her arms were crossed over her chest. Her eyes were pinned. "Renata," I said, and Nina looked toward the hall to her left, still saying nothing.

"You get her the hell out of here," Moses said. "Don't say anything about her, just get her to the hospital, and don't come back here. You were never here."

"We'll take care of you for this," Nina said.

Lloyd and I ran down the hall to Renata. She was hardly breathing, and little flecks of foam had gathered on her lips. All

I remember Lloyd saying was, "Oh, fuck." We carried her out be-
tween us and got her into the van. Lloyd said not to lay her down
but keep her sitting up, so we propped her between us on the
front seat and screamed over to the close hospital on the West
Side. Moses had something right again—we couldn't stay there.
We brought her inside and told the receptionist that she wasn't
breathing, which was almost accurate. When two men came out
between some swinging doors and trotted over to her, Lloyd and
I quickly slipped away.

I phoned Nina the next day, but she did not answer, and when
I went up to her building the doorman told me no one was there
and not to come back until I got a call, which came the next day.
"She's dead," Nina said. "We are going to take care of everything.
I'm going to leave an envelope for you. It's complicated. Don't
come back. The police will be looking for you. You should go
away for a while. The other guy too."

"Lloyd," I said.

"I don't need to know who he is."

"In the envelope, then," I said. "Lloyd gets something. It was
his van."

"I don't know anything about a van," Nina said. Neither of us
spoke for a second, then she said, "There'll be enough for both
of you."

"What about Renata?" I asked. But she hung up.

There are no notes or narratives after that. Lloyd took the
money—I gave him mine, too—and Far Rockaway left for San
Francisco. I avoided jail by surrendering to the draft board with
terms and conditions. I could choose the navy and even be a
journalist. The latter turned out to be a lie. They sent me to the
middle of the war. When I came back the world was different. I
lived a number of different lives. Nothing that happened before

the war even seemed real to me anymore. But that turned out to be not true either.

In November of 2015 I received an email from one of my editors letting me know that someone named Ana Bento Lewis had written, asking for my email or phone number, and would it be all right to give them to her. I had not seen Ana since our last summer in town. I had been in Provincetown a few times for the Portuguese Festival since then and had asked some old friends about her. She had been to town to the festival herself once or twice it seems, but we never made it back in the same year. She'd asked about me too, and that's how information got passed to one another—chatting with others during the party weekend. I learned that she had married Rafael Lewis, an immigration attorney, and that they lived in Canada. She worked as a graphic designer and also kept a small studio where she painted watercolors and made small sculptures out of wire. I am unabashedly not on any social media, so those channels were not open, and the truth is that once we parted after high school, we were never good at keeping in touch.

Ana had left for college a week or two before I left for New York. As I think back now, I cannot remember a falling-out between us, but neither do I remember our saying anything to each other before we went our separate ways. No goodbyes. And I never thought about how much influence Renata might have had on Ana's life too. That rare force. There was somehow money for her to go off to college, and she did. She also wanted something more than the town. As it turned out during our phone conversations, it came up that we each harbored feelings, opaque to us at the time, about the other's prospects. Ana wanted to do something bold, like go to San Francisco or Los Angeles, but she was bound for UMass Amherst with her small scholarship and other help, and the Bentos were adamant. She saw me as somehow free and independent and resented it. As in an O. Henry story, I was angry at how she left me abruptly, and how she was able to go to a university and I could not. We were still children for all our efforts at being cool. But we both carried something of Renata with us. She had turned us on to this idea that a world was out there buzzing with possibility and risk. We saw her living on an edge, sometimes dangerous. But you had to keep moving. Going nowhere was a kind of death. That was Renata. That was what she was to us. Don't get trapped.

After our initial emails, we spent a good deal of time during several phone calls just clearing things up. We laughed a lot at our young selves. We caught up. We reminisced. We had had good times together. We spent a lot of time talking about Renata, too. She had fit into our psyches, for each of us in different ways, but what was common about it was the space she had occupied, which we revisited after all these years. So much Renata.

But now Ana's news was that her sister Rosa had died, and Ana had come down from Toronto, where she and her husband now lived. She was in the process of settling things. Mrs. Bento had passed away eleven years ago, and Rosa had cleaned out the old house and sold it. She had taken quite a bit of stuff from the house with her back up the Cape to her own home in Chatham, where she had lived by herself. Now Rosa was gone, too soon, Ana said. She had died after what was supposed to have been a routine surgery. Ana didn't go into details. But in Rosa's cellar in Chatham were two boxes—big wooden fish boxes from the old Cold Storage. And they were filled with Renata's things. I asked how this could possible, and Ana told me that Renata had come back to Provincetown for a while sometime in the mid-1980s. Maybe '85 or '86. "That can't be," I said.

"Oh, I know exactly what you're going to say. She died. But that's not what happened. Renata told me all about it. I came down for a week just to be with her and my mother. Mãe was just thrilled to see her. Renata talked about you. You saved her the night she almost died in New York, right? Anyway, she got into big trouble from that and went to jail for it. They thought she was dealing drugs or something like that. She was going to have to go trial, but some people bailed her out. Here's the cool deal. It was all set up. They bailed her out, but she was supposed to jump bail and disappear. That was the deal. Disappear. They were okay with that. They knew they were going to lose the money. Actually, you know, they wanted her gone. They gave her money to leave the country too, and rigged some sort of deal about that also. But you know how she used to be. Renata, I mean. She could make a good story out of anything, but that's pretty much the gist of what she told me. It was those Hammond people, which you knew. They were the ones. I guess you worked for them. She told me all about it, and she talked about you a lot. She was happy that you were doing well, but I didn't have that much to tell her. Well, you know how that goes. But she looked good. Same Renata, but gray hair. Good shape. Still slim. Pretty with a few wrinkles. She stayed with Mãe for a month or more, and then she asked to store some things because she had to go to someplace. I only got this from Mãe—I was gone already—but she said some place in Africa. She didn't know how long she would be gone, but she planned to come back to town eventually. You just couldn't tell with Renata. You know her passport said Renée Farrar on it? She never came back. Mãe either didn't know or couldn't remember the name of the place she was going to. She might have had Africa wrong, for all that, because when I had talked to Renata, she mentioned Italy. Where the volcano buried all those people. Not Pompeii but the other one. Herculaneum. Who knows? You know Mãe. But she just kept everything for Renata like she said she would."

We had a few more phone conversations like this one. Bits and pieces about the old days, about Renata, which helped my memory of those early years. We spoke fondly of our young times together. I was in some kind of shock, of course. How some things are never over.

But what came of all this was that in one of the boxes was an old typewriter in a smaller black box with a bunch of papers laid across the top of the machine. There was a note inside that said, *This is for Frankie, meu Coitado. whenever you see him. Diga-lhe que eu gosto da cabeça dele!* I told Ana I would fly back east to get the box right way, and that anyway it would be good to see her again, but she said no, she had to get back to Canada in a few days, and she would send it out to me. I asked her to send it the fastest way possible, C.O.D. or however it would get to me quickly with my paying the cost. The box, the old Underwood, and Renata's manuscript along with some other papers arrived at my home in Los Angeles in two days.

II.

Renata's manuscript in its original form comprised fifty-two poems, interspersed with two pages of the poet's notes, and displaying five epigraphs. This volume follows exactly the organization and sequence of these original pages. The poems themselves are gathered in three separate sections, each section with a single-word subtitle and epigraph. The pages were typed on inexpensive paper, a kind of newsprint cut to a standard 8½ x 11 format. A routine search of paper manufacturing by types and sizes has yielded no compelling evidence as to whether the paper was produced in Portugal or the United

States. The text itself shows many strikeovers and, in places, parts of lines or whole lines are struck through with replacement words typed beneath, or sometimes appearing at the bottom of the page with an arrow drawn back to the overstrike, indicating the placement of the substitution. Some lines were struck through without replacement, which the editors read as intentional deletions. It has been suggested that an original version of the poems might have been written in Portuguese, with Renata typing an English version afterward, but there is no evidence yet of a Portuguese-language text. Furthermore, there is no evidence of any of the individual poems having been published in any form either in English or Portuguese, though it is likely that some may have been passed hand to hand.

If the poems give a reasonable account of her activities, then Renata used an Olivetti machine when working on clandestine material in Lisbon. Perhaps, as a means of caution, she wrote this book on my typewriter, the 1936 Underwood portable. Aside from the fact that we shared this machine at one time, and that Renata certainly (amazingly) returned it to me with the poems, a simple test of the typeface confirms this.

Renata Ferreira's work has been heretofore unknown, and the circumstances of its appearance at this time in the corpus of Portuguese-American literature are as surprising as they are remarkable. This collection of poems, by virtue of its distinctive voice and its passionate accounts of love and danger during the tumultuous days before Portugal's Carnation Revolution, positions her as one of the essential Portuguese-American poets of the mid-twentieth century. Although her work was hidden away for at least forty years, its absence from readership and discussion nearly symbolizes another absence: the dearth of critical attention and commercial distribution of Portuguese-American writing in this country's mainstream literary culture, either through lack of interest, condescension, or little awareness that such a literature exists at all. As fortuitous as the discovery of Renata's work might be, the fact that it comes to us in a time of continuing literary marginalization makes its very appearance in print at least one small advance on the gatekeepers, one puissant arrow in the wall.

Although Renata's poetry is rooted in Eros, in its many forms, in aggregate she winds our way through her days and nights in the underground of Lisbon during the end times of Portugal's fascist state. It is important to note that Renata does not write as commentator or historian. She is a poet and visual artist: everything in this book is written from her particular and distinct point of view. Even as she was an important member of the general resistance as a pamphleteer and *rescriptor* of banned material, her distinctive style in this volume gives voice to her heart, her psyche, her struggles in love and passion, and her unabashed sexuality, which she declares is her sovereign ground of subversion. Though the primal driving force here is erotic, she is by turns meditative, profane, reverent, funny, paratactic, and allusive.

Markedly, Renata opens the book with an epigraph from Sappho's own fragment no. 1, sometimes called "Song to Aphrodite," and she follows quickly with a poem that establishes the context for her own ardors and complications: "Island," which we understand is the unnamed Lesbos, and addresses her erstwhile lover, Anaktoria, also the name of the young girl whose unexplained absence Sappho herself lamented. We will see that every poem in this book, declared or not, is addressed to Renata's own lover, whose physical reality we are sometimes moved to question (although some scenes render her clearly as a flesh and blood object of ardent attention). Renata may have had a number of reasons to name her lover Anaktoria, the possible shading of the woman's identity being at least one of them. But as we move through the poems, we must never underinterpret Renata. None of her importance is unmerited.

Sappho famously in fragment no. 16 talks lovingly of the young
girl:

> Some say an army of horsemen, others
> say foot soldiers, still other say a fleet
> is the finest thing on the dark earth.
> I say it is the one you love.

And later,

> . . . there are things that remind me now
> of Anaktoria, and I for one would rather see
> her supple step and the sparkle on her face
> then watch all the dazzling chariots and
> and armored soldiers of Lydia.

For chariots in this day, we may well read tanks or armored
personnel carriers, but this poem is a key to Sappho's adumbrating
her claim that the lyric poem, with its songlike (and sung) verses
of shorter measure, is equal in dignity to the grand if ponderous
hexameters of the epics. In declaring this she opens the dialectic
between the two poetic impulses of her day. To be sure she is
not the first lyric poet—Archilochos (also of Lesbos) preceded
her with some repute, but how many of us have heard of him?
Plato might have, but in his highest praise he said memorably
that Sappho was "the tenth muse." And Sappho, most of whose
work comes to us in fragments and tatters or is altogether lost,
remains one of the most powerful women in the world. And she
stands toe to toe with Homer and never gives an inch.

What has this to do with Renata? Renata reveres her certainly,
but getting back to the dichotomy that Sappho announces in
her Anaktoria poem, we watch Renata very purposefully have

it both ways. And she knows just what she is doing. Her individual poems, radical though they are, all in one way or another become songs of love or lament, or longing: that is, lyric. But the collection as a whole arcs itself into a staccato narrative that so adeptly treats her time and place as epic that in the final poem of the book she has to declare that it is not one. Though she sometimes assumes a naïve voice, there is nothing basic or accidental about this woman's art.

As I use the word *naïve* another somewhat mysterious woman comes to mind, and though she may seem distantly appropriated I will name her: Emily Dickinson. The access of her work to publication and serious critical attention was in part impeded by what editors saw as primitive attempts at competence with the rhyme and the standard meters of its day. Though not a great deal can be made of a strict comparison of their lives and work, a discussion of the fracturing of technique in their respective poetry might offer some insight into where authentic style originates and how it manifests itself in a poet's signal work. And we don't have to push too hard to see a few basic similarities in the two women. Both find their hearts harried and imprisoned by love, and their lives for better or for worse are bent into extraordinary shapes by this. They each address an absent lover—Anaktoria for Renata and The Master for Dickinson. Their absences may be geographical or emotional or even the result of restrictive cultural or political considerations. And neither poet's work quite resembles the standard modes of utterance of its time. One might attribute this to a proclivity for artistic innovation and a search for new methods of expression, but certainly Dickinson was no enfant terrible of the avant garde. An easier case might be made for Renata in that light, but I think the character of these poets and the characteristics of their verse point to other reasons: the extreme demands they encountered in the expression of their respective sexuality, the spiritual aloneness that we see break through in some of their most moving poems, and the almost religious longing for answers to the impossible questions that they continually pose to themselves all serve to press upon their thought and sensation, and they must burst forth in forms that established prosody cannot accommodate—indeed that language itself may not sufficiently accommodate.

In Dickinson's case, she altered received forms to fit her personal utterance. She found rhyme that seemed to satisfy her in places where other people could hear none. She employs words in places and with usages that no one seems to have thought of before. She developed her own idiosyncratic system of punctuation. And for all the repression that may have constricted her life, her mind was forbidden access to no place or subject, regardless of how innocent or trivial her verse sounded to the uninitiated reader.

Renata was not the supernova that Dickinson was. No one is. Yet I find that the character of Renata's work indicates similar extreme pressures in Renata's psyche, and I read her distinctive style also as a bursting forth of those pressures into the only forms she could devise to express them.

Whereas Dickinson wrestles and cages her lines into new fashion, Renata seems to plunge headfirst through the argument of hers. Her lines do not break but bend, and her rhythmic foot may be measured in an expanse of a thought as easily as a duration of a sound. Renata does not really invent her own system of punctuation; she nearly abjures punctuation altogether. And the subject of a poem as often as not turns out to be nothing the reader could possibly expect from its beginning, yet the poem hangs together as though it were ordained to do so. Like Dickinson, her mind too is forbidden nothing; she is bold in her aesthetic and cultural transgressions.

Regarding the element of transgression in Renata's poems, it is helpful to consider two other poets, one Portuguese, one American. Florbela Espanca was born in Vila Viçosa, Portugal, in 1894, and Edna St. Vincent Millay, two years earlier in 1892, in Rockland, Maine. Both poets shared the early years of the twentieth century and the world as it developed and changed after the Great War. Their cultures were, of course, vastly different, yet I do not think any seasoned reader can think of one poet without considering the other. Both poets were iconoclastic, transgressive, flamboyant in personality, and nearly always in love or lamenting its loss. And both used the vehicle of the sonnet as a principal means of expression. Both were masters of the form.

Florbela preferred the Italian sonnet (and its variations), the eight-and-six of da Lentini and Camões; Millay wrote her sonnets almost exclusively in the English form. These distinctions are not simply matters of style but matters of expression. The Italian, with its sestet answering the octet, orients itself toward dialectic, call and response; its energy occurs in the transport between the two sections. The English sonnet allows Millay to accrue her argument consecutively through three quatrains and bring the poem to a definitive close with the final couplet. Millay's closures are dazzling.

Florbela's rhymes are deft and beautifully sonorous in the Portuguese. Without these, in English, we tend to focus on the structure of the stanzas and the poem as a whole. Florbela often fractures the octet and the sestet into smaller units and varies their content, giving the reader a sense of almost four different poems in one, and multiplying their energetic stanza breaks.

What distinguishes these writers as a pair is that they both reach back over centuries to an established, proven form, easily identified as legitimate in their respective cultures. But each poet, stretching then breaking standard boundaries (certainly the boundaries given to women writers) with expressions of their sexuality, their intensity of passion, and their bold posture brings newness to the form and to the voice of women talking about their deepest desires and regrets. There are those cultural differences, of course, between the language of Florbela and the language of Millay, but there is no retreating from the ground gained by them.

Renata is clearly in their theater of expression: sex, desire, disappointment, deep feelings, and a superlative articulation of those feelings *that are always linked to thought.* In some lush fantasy the three of them could sit in a comfortable café and talk for endless nights. What a conversation that might be! Renata, though, does not use, nor need to use, accepted forms for her poems. She writes luxuriously in that twilight of modernism that we have only weakly managed to name *post*modernism. As such she is free to invent her own kind of wildness, and we, in our own time, are used to discovering new expressions of wildness. Renata is never confusing, always clear and readable, yet often her calls and responses each seem to belong to their own disparate poems. Frequently her gradual accrual is splintered and blazes the reader into completely new territory. Nearly all her closures are worked toward the emphatic and definitive. If we agree that these features are in themselves formal, as we witness in Millay and Florbela, then we can isolate them as talismans from the long traditions of poetry, distributed in the whirlwinds of Renata's work.

But none of this is to say that Renata isn't conversant or skilled in actual formal verse. There is always form in her poems; they *are* form. And she does seem to plant a couple of "Easter eggs" in her book to demonstrate what she knows to the careful reader. Her one eight-and-six sonnet "wild" is a strong example of the octet and the sestet creating a surprising field of energy between them. Although she does not use rhyme in that sonnet, she flaunts her skill with it (and tells us so) in the cautionary "absinthe."

Renata's work in this collection overflows with allusions, pastiches, slyly placed bits of quotations, and references to a wide range of authors: from Clarice Lispector to D. H. Lawrence, from Walt Whitman to Fernando Pessoa (look for a cameo appearance by the disguised master), from Allen Ginsberg to Luis de Camões, from the Three Marias to Soror Mariana, and ever more, on and on. Her experiences range from New York to Lisbon, from Ponta Delgada to Provincetown, and who knows how far beyond. Both Portugal and America are home to her. She is tenant to the daemon of each. She is rustic, she is cosmopolitan, she is restless, she is turbulent, she is native, she is peregrine, and no matter where or how she makes landfall, she manages to shape an easeful home in her own skin.

III.

Although Renata's collection develops its own context as the reader moves forward in the poems (reading them in order, front to back, best illustrates their arc), some background about their time and setting may ease entry into the book's multifold world. With that in mind, I offer the following brief gloss of place and event for interested readers, and endnotes will also extend or supplement material in the poems.

Modern Portugal gradually came under the dictatorship of Antonio Salazar in the late 1920s and early '30s. Salazar established himself as a strongman nationalist, and his new government, known as *O Estado Novo*, "The New State," sought order and progress via tight moral and social control of its citizens.

Estado Novo exhibited the salient features of fascism: corpora-
tions and government were closely allied in purpose, unions
were persecuted, the free press was attacked and abrogated,
books, films, and periodicals were heavily censored or banned
outright; dissidents were summarily arrested and imprisoned,
often beaten, and sexual activity was dictated by the most strin-
gently conservative precepts of the Catholic Church. Women did
not have full political or legal equality with men, and access to
divorce, contraception, and in many cases higher education was
restricted. Same-sex activity was deemed invisible and therefore
nonexistent in Estado Novo, and yet if witnessed it was liable to
criminal prosecution.

An admirer of Benito Mussolini and Adolf Hitler, Salazar
modeled his secret police, the dreaded Polícia Internacional e
de Defesa do Estado (PIDE) after the SS, and designed his one
concentration camp, Tarrafal, in the Cape Verde Islands, after
German prototypes. Throughout this time, hundreds of citizens
were pressed to become paid government informants, watching
for any suspicious or threatening activity and dampening any
sense of domestic freedom.

It is fair to say that Salazar was seen by some as a savior of the
country, deftly steering Portugal though a precarious neutral-
ity during World War II and avoiding much of the catastrophic
turmoil and damage experienced by other European countries.
His devout and rigid Catholicism was taken to exhibit moral
imperatives and social mores. In the earliest days of his admin-
istration he did help to stabilize and even strengthen Portugal's
parlous economy, but after the war the country fell into stagna-
tion and was left behind during Europe's general reconstruction
and modernization. The proscriptions and fascist government
controls continued, and the policy of "tropicalization," and the
seemingly endless colonial wars in Africa and Asia, bled the

already ailing social and economic body politic. Thousands of young men were drafted into service in these foreign conflicts; thousands more fled the country to avoid conscription. This is to say nothing about the damage of the wars themselves, the attempted subjugation of native peoples, the killing and atrocities on all sides, and the general sense of futility that fogged Portugal.

Salazar suffered a stroke in 1968, and his ministers quietly removed him from his offices, isolating him from the government, but through a ruse allowed him to think he was still in control. His place was taken by Marcelo Caetano, who promised some degree of liberalization, but these pledges never materialized in any significant way. By the 1970s, the country was ripe for upheaval.

Renata Ferreira

I have more than one soul.
There are more I's than I myself.
—ricardo reis

Eh-lá, eh-lá, eh-lá, bazar o meu coração.
—álvaro de campos

anaktoria

what thing I long for to appease my frantic
soul, and who must I now persuade, you ask,
who must untangle your love and who now,
sappho, has wronged you

island

anaktoria you can feel her young her smooth her
long muscles, her hair like the wet stones, her thicket
even blacker naked in the sunlight, it makes me choke
a sob in the jail of my own bones trying to get it out
and so much missing in that yellow book you gave me
fragments tatters, where did all those pieces disappear to

the roof beams here have been lowered the ceiling sweats
the defects, the bloom, you won't be young again
the girls you pined for will stay young forever, you
don't have a song for them, your legs ache you say
what's next you say, what shape were those sails,
that's what you wrote in pencil at the bottom of a page

all I see is an island a shore the sand bright in the sun
you see this is that trance you call love, it does them
no good, they no longer love, our queen and her girls,
you are trying to tell me something, you are saying
all that yearning is now for me, for you, for whoever will
allow it, you can see she left us with some kind of wound

noose

yes but what anyone suspects here is immaterial
utterly stupid and still the world sits on it all
like a hill of nails, any manner of love is the last
thing the state should think of when it's all money
and guns and jungles and those fat brown tanks

I am their most dangerous enemy with my mouth
on my lover, as you were I am being careful with
my insurgencies but I will overcome everything,
those sober faces will whiten and die just like
you and I will, they act like they don't know it

in a shop today dust and paper and pens
I bought a glass that makes things larger
I looked at the dead flies along the windowsill,
they draw near to gemstones the blue and green
the black, after a while I did not want to see them
except blown close like the machines that they are
it didn't make me sad how small the world is

and then at night with the light bulbs struggling
on their wire noose, the gutter dogs singing, I
tried to write down their language, there were no
words but sober howling, how foolish at the table
with all the pencils, if this quarter moon were a sea
we'd all vanish right here among the green mermaids
when you must always beware of someone watching you
it is a way to feel safe behind the noise and the troubles

knot

sometimes when the moon is right
it presents your shadow to me
mostly the moon is not right,
where are you laying your head,
I am not asking for anything

from a bench in the park
I watch the automobiles their color
and their speed seem the same thing
there is no behind in a life, behind
keeps spooling in the dark like the cinema

I remember my mother saying
how handsome salazar was and then
some kind of trouble, my father sent us
away america brazil I never saw him again
I was so small, I might be making this up,
it's the way other people's stories slip
into your head, you try not to own them

you slept in the bedroom with jungle boots on
you are always there, moonlight, electric light
what do you know about aching for a touch
anaktoria, I baked a custard, I wore your
green apron, I kept wiping my hands on it
I could not undo the knot to get it off me

swans

sun finally on the shelves, sun on the cast-iron sink
sun after the gray days of fog and the long bells
from the river, I can open a book, all the clocks stop
I admire the books, they were not put in the world
to be fucked or weep in the mornings for no reason
even though they keep all that inside themselves,
they love me best, I can read and fall asleep in the sun
the book will surrender and settle on my chest

bathing at the sink, smelling hot bread and coffee
you came behind me and squeezed lemon on your hands
you won't remember this yet, you held the hair up off my neck
and washed with the warm cloth all down my back
which is not untrue if I can get you to do it sooner or later

it's prophecy then, I make the future, my god is the god of
        swans,
socrates smiled when he said that, your god is the god
of the body, the weather how the wet seeps into
some books, I open to dry their damp pages on the windowsill
and then they are meadows in the sunlight
no government can refute this, how I admire the window
how the glass panes allow so much to pass
I admire you I can't help it, you come into any room
as though you belong there no matter what, it's the way
sometimes my teeth clench without my even knowing it

wedge

people talk they find out things
you have to be ready someone is
already willing to betray you even
if it's just for your face or that
you wear glasses or they know
you won't sneak into their homes
and murder them although I would,
I remember in school that passage
the crusaders wading in blood
to their horses' knees, oh wonder

I was unwell once for a long time
it felt like I was stone and rope
I dressed before my mirror over
and over combinations of fur
and wool and silk and then naked
naked that's why I told you our
souls serve only our cunts, you
didn't like the word and then you
did when I said it meant wedge

it is a simple machine like the
pulley or the wheel without which
the earth would be barren of all
inventions, I explained this to a man
outside the library he was afraid
to go in, he said he thought the police
were watching him, little man, there must

be thousands of them, dark suit tie
hat glasses everything worn and frayed

I brought him home, up the stairs
I filled a grocery bag with books
for him, many of them were yours
it's just one of those acts, you think
you are saving something somewhere,
he kept saying no, no, no I can't then
in the end he took them but he saw
my table the fliers the stacks the olivetti
now I am afraid he was a government spy
tell me if it was right that I did this

bone

you don't choose your soul, my soul
is too much like my body, opaque and
bony it casts a shadow like any wall

not clear, transparent never, this time and place
is where a creature like me circles before
she sits, my face is a proscenium, nothing
moving in front of that curtain is what it seems

it's a good life, I sharpen on the rocks like a razor
I rub my edge to sleep on the troubles,
you were created dear one just as I was

women who love women must not be found
in the new state because unseen they will not exist
old man salazar said so himself with his purple mouth
caetano keeps it alive in his withered sack of edicts

oh let's go down to the old bridge and watch the bats
pitch and scissor while the stars come up from under,
the bats like clouds rising black then blacker

then won't you and I be like a pair of candles
but with no altar bone no saint just a mirror
of oil on the water, just our two hands holding on

peru

all my ideas are antique like my rouge
I read that horrid book you gave me
rouge on her nipples the lips shackles men
whipped her fucked her everywhere for years
she thought it was love she begged for death
why is it a game always, whips and beatings for
the effete and privileged who invent submission
while our women here trudge smothered in black coats
why delight in the misery of so many, how else
would you say it, I know how you say it, don't
draw blood with the knives of what you desire

also life is an exclusive club all leather
chairs and a lucky footman tending the hearth
so look, you and I and all these others we
were let in, we are sisters in the pedigree
but I feel dark about it all like something
is brooding at the edges of the city, pale bricks
and wrecking balls swinging with nobody near them

why don't we just behave like other people
you see them walking they are all fine on
the outside, that's all you ever know and when
it rains, the future is even brighter, it seems
like everyone salutes one another the way
they hurtle under their black umbrellas

you must not prognosticate, I wrote it on
the mirror with a tube of lipstick which
is not at all rouge, I go through the little
embroidered bag you gave me from peru
I stir around with my fingers trying to
come up with what I need, a sharp file, little
scissors, lampblack for the singed eyebrows
sometimes I turn it over and dump it all on
the glass table, something is always missing

list

I have a fever, anaktoria, I do not keep
my own prescriptions, it is gray
now here in lisbon, there is no cure for
love, because when someone loves you
she always wants something

I sat in the window again
this time breathing the fog
where does it go when it goes
I like how the whistles and horns
travel through it, it is the lateness
of the hour that keeps me from burning

you are confused when I think about you
you walk with a limp
your coat is long and black
you are always running back from something

I don't care, I bought some roses
and cut their heads off and floated them
in a bowl, they tipped on their sides,
I am frantic mad, and restless
I will make a list for you in pencil
the things I wanted to do with you
It's very late I do not know all their names

leather

don't you see I never talk about anything except paradise
it's not the party or the unions but I can no longer explain
myself, it's like trying to dream in a language I've never heard,
I don't mean dream like longing or need

your face anaktoria when I told you how they questioned me
they kept me for two days they watched me piss in a bucket,
I said I needed the wind in the kitchen because it's the opposite
of kiss, they took a valise of my translations, bills, inventories, orders
descriptions of propellers hulls rudders, complaints, marine glass
also my own receipts for this work, they found only legal, they
tried to act like they knew something, two men who could only
read the portuguese parts, I am supposed to be afraid now

when I write bulletins about the three marias I say they are
entombed and still beaten which is not necessarily the truth
but it translates well, today they will go to france and belgium
and then pamphlets will be picked up, you know who I mean

what else love, I am being careful but all my air slips by
too easily, where does it go, it pitches me down a green
corridor with lamps burning like little fevers, do you see
it's never enough, your face when I told you, became someone
else's face, with the eyes of that woman who looks like leather
and sits in the doorway of the bank and holds her hand out
for coins when people walk by and try not to look at her

radio

I get lonesome when you're away and I'm not fucking you,
it's not what you think, I can tell what you think by your
face and where you put your hands, even when your hands
are around my heart you are away

I like the street here, there is only room for one small car
at a time, at night the young people settle in the bars
and fill the sidewalks, you know informants are among them
I watch them like they are a different species, the pipes sputter
I save water in a pot, I bathe over the kitchen sink

I am not responsible, things were done to me, you can't
trap me into carrying those bloody rags around, all my shame
is really your shame, my body is a desert, my mind is its storm,
no one crosses me, no one can get over
I have had to learn how to wait

the fountains in the square are as white as soap
but there is no water in them, leaves and bits of paper
collect, caetano is censoring war news on the radio again,
we don't hear anything that is the truth, today I fried
a fish from the river it came wrapped in the diário

it's not about fucking you, it's just what I think about,
blue door, the eleven steps up, the dead plumbing, I am
not trying to say that I missed you all day, I listened to
the radio, it kept saying my name, how does a radio
work, a little green box on the kitchen table

do you hear music in your head, two lines of a song over
and over, do you move according to them all day

I am judith and you are holofernes
but sometimes we change, it's the other way around
your fingers, your tongue, your shoes on the landing,
I have a small knife, I am going to use it to unscrew
the back of the radio, I am going to empty it of all those
wires inside and spread them on the tablecloth, then
we can be shy and sit together and look for all the voices

sheets

I could run to johannesburg or maybe rome
however the trains go, I could take one suitcase
I could make tea over an alcohol stove, I could
sleep with my head on the shoulders of unknown
men and women, my new breath would smell like bread

why don't you want to hear this, I have my own fate
I have an empty book with colored pencils, I have maps
that I have drawn myself, and the olivetti a sister
would keep for me until I came home again, morocco
prague, you understand, sappho said her lover
was more beautiful than all the hoplites of lydia but
how did she know, what armies did she ride among

as if the armies haven't always been gathered,
as if the wars were really art and splendor, I can't
funnel you into any of the necessary categories, it
is always, I, I, I, you, you, you, and then we have to
compare damage, you cannot choose not to love me
you said that, why is that force so terrible, you stepping
out of the grey vagão on the tracks in cais do sodré
but you remind me that that never happened, and so
why do I remember it, your handkerchief, your loose
trousers, your slouch hat, your furled umbrella so black

just because it's raining, just because all I can hear
is the roof jumping and the gutter spouts, the streets
become streams, I won't dream, you will be wet and cold

when you come in, I will take your clothes off and lay
them on the table and dry you in my sheets, your body,
that's how it will go, that's how it will always go, you'll see

quicksilver

think of your life without all those narcissistic traumas
or would there be anything left to keep you walking upright
I went out to the café rosa for a hot galáo from
one of those tall glasses you like, it was just at that hour
when you feel the dusk on your skin like an oiled hand

I don't ask, I know exactly why I'm here, I don't
think about becoming nothing, I think it's impractical
I smoked a cigarette, I bought another notebook with blue
and red lines, how do you suppose you can leave your
traces in a thing like that then someday fail to exist

you exist in my mind which is sometimes better than in
my flat or in my bathtub, sometimes I am lead sometimes
you are quicksilver, when I am a statue so are you but
don't you think really we are just two ends of the whip
exchanging places, what is wrong with you, you are like
a weak chin with your abstinence, don't you ever think
that we breed our lies and wear our masks just to survive,
of course it becomes a habit, that's where we all get so lost

jump

you ought to stop with all your opinions
say my name, you never know what might occur
the floors sometimes shift out of kilter
there's a board that moans, for a minute
I feel a swoon in my head like the whole building
will spiral to ruin, I have become used to this,
it's one of those visitations that have turned friendly

don't understand me too quickly dear sister in chains,
you are always the knock on the door, the draft in the room
imagine london, the lover there is always like the weather
or poppies or roses, what are you in lisbon then, henna,
hemp, a weed in a crack in the marble of the roman baths

there is a drug I love, it is like nothing but itself
it makes my letters jump and then pleasure
it can turn the spies to ash and the police to vapor
it lets you see right through another's clothes
and then squander, I would sleep with anyone,

then all the roses and their cousins are the shadows
under my feet, I study rebellion in all my languages,
you'll see what I mean, when you tell me my heart
is loud and wayward why would I ever listen to you
you are the one who laid the fire in my ears

notas

avante, stockholm bulletin, luta, frente patriótica de libertação naciona
because you do not have your own manifesto

today a boy was arrested for having a battery-powered radio
he was stripped in the square the crowd refused to look at him

you are all the dead and all the living and the world you feel the strugg
for a book must not teach the world but only how to be portuguese

a woman named no one has stolen documents from a high office
the pamphlet and bulletin are the blades below the fourth rib

over the darkness of the shining roofs the cold light of morning break
mist or smoke was it rising from the earth or falling from the sky

margarida held a soldier's hand for hours in the rossio he was so scare
if the resistance fails I will continue in the hours love and defy

for our salazar learned firsthand from the germans
tarrafal in cape verde the pide in the streets of lisbon

the dead only weep that carnal love must be weaponized
for holy lent I once gave you up for an hour

for the laipis azul is the leech of truth
for purple ink will betray the source as cópias de carbono strike be

let them ignore the enemy within the gate
while they search for another so far away

the yeast of life are my secrets only if I keep them sacred
I have earned all my fate so will you

miguel and alma from the train with suitcases
they visit the women beyond the city dutch caps and jelly

let miguel know to rotate the tape machine to me the same way
I will transcribe that broadcast a voz da liberdade from algiers

este caderno não pertence a ninguém
if you find this you will not find the others nor the others think about it

wing

what if I translated skylark or nightingale
into bird just bird, if I changed everything
that naming does, so what if adam did it,
don't you agree, isn't the tree of life more
than the tree of life without a label for the
fruit, we have bananas and oranges this
morning tell me the difference, last night
in the rosa I told a girl to close her eyes,
I said thrush pigeon tercel, tell me what
you see I said, I only hear words she said,
she wouldn't kiss me it's the age difference

You hold the knife and I'll hold the gun, we'll
write a song together, I love you, you love me
I don't care who you kiss, your hair is like sun
on the back of a crow, your lips are the graze
of an arrow your smell is just the way I twitched
inside even across the crowded room, sometimes
such a faint rumor of what we laid at each other's
feet, I can call it a bird because it slants the air
like a wing does, breathe deep anaktoria I don't
know how much longer any of us can last

rosa

rosa's was crowded I didn't see the woman
I was supposed to meet, I carried twenty 3-fold
bulletins in my bag, how you would fold them
for me sometimes so accurate and press them
flat, something was not right I looked for a trap
but the room seemed the same as always the girls
wanted love, sex was out the window, who was
burning your candle now, I sat by the doorway

there was talk at the table, a woman was saying
africa africa someone's brother was killed in angola
he was so small a girl said, that helmet, and that rifle
was so big hanging on him he looked like a child playing,
they were passing a photograph, I didn't try to look,
they were drinking gingina I could see the street
the pide was out, they kept passing, everyone should
have been more afraid, too much talk too much music
too many women, rosa sat at the counter smoking

one week now and the café is gone, newspaper over
the windows a heavy board across the door

no one has seen rosa no word among the sisters yet
we are hoping a night train, marseille or salzburg

scream

you wake up every morning it's the ruined kingdom
you punish yourself you make coffee before dawn
I look along the rooftops and out to the river
your face says you were born for something better
I didn't cheat you out of anything I won't open my pockets
I'm sick of trying to get to the bottom of love

one voice in my mouth is false another has no taste
sometimes I want an axe and a long boat to kill from,
let the fascists scream, love is something beyond me
outside me, brutality, a tropism to the rapture
when I am first struck by it, but in every account
I mark it down, I will tell you disaster, debris

if you take all the stairs below and then the cellar
rows of clouded jars, the shelves, mold, stale water
spiders clicking along old chains rusted in the corner
you should come down with me, the air tastes like corruption
I will terrify you, I am the monstrosity I try to describe
but you don't even know how dark it gets here, sometimes
I cry in broad daylight because you don't know how dark

ophelia

There's rosemary, that's for remembrance; pray,
love, remember; and there is pansies, that's for
thoughts. . . . There's fennel for you, and colum-
bines; there's rue for you, and here's some for me; we
may call it herb of grace o' Sundays. O, you must
wear your rue with a difference.

girls

I cannot find the name of the woman
who was burned at the stake in 1935
somewhere outside lisbon, I cannot find the name
of the woman who was shot and killed by police
for demanding a raise during the early strikes,
you can go through the papers in the archives
but the censors, whole paragraphs pages
missing, it means something those girls
could have been you or me, the newspapers
are images on plastic you pull them through
a machine there's a smell like vinegar

I am breathless and spoiled with mirages
think of an acid that could burn the suffering
out of love, you could see it on a laboratory table
like shrapnel, the misery, you put it in a beaker
or someone carries it away in a steaming bucket
and then what's left is the joy which is supposed
to be heaven but even in the mind this does not work
you understand your devils singing inside after a while

there are things now that I would not do for you
but when I consider they are not many

forget the stores lining the streets with candles
rosaries, fátima dinner plates, missals porcelain angels
there were never women angels in the scriptures but
in the shops they make the little statues into girls

and then angels are not so terrifying, you can pick them
up like toy skylarks and make them fly over the counters
imagine gabriel with his pale hand on poor mary's belly
you know in your heart it's not there to comfort

wild

there was a little grass yard behind the chapel
we would practice our kissing on one another
the nuns must have been waiting, they flew at us like kites
they said they would send us to the monsignor for caning
but instead made us kneel on stones and recite the confiteor
until we ached, knees and backs, after a while you forget
what the words mean, you just ache and cry, what
were we supposed to signify, it was a good prayer

    sayeth the lord, who does not abide with me and
don't you know the lord sayeth to stone the woman,
he tells us in what manner she is to be beaten
or cast out, sometimes you remind me of jesus when
you gather the women around you, but jesus went
with the wild girl, I hope you are following all this

veil

you are a subject I cannot exhaust
you say all your faults are my projections
but projections make me think of the cinema
you know there were two girls that day two
and you regarded each other by pretending
each was air and it came down to you, we
looked at the poster beautiful in stark inks
a man in a fedora, a wide-eyed woman but
you were the coming attraction and I still
hear from that other girl, young and dark
and always in bad fortune, I don't know
why the bed was so wet and bloody
that night you were so happy, laughing
while you were coming, it is raining
here and I am drowsy watching the water
boil for coffee, I am going to crush some
pills later and rub them on my tongue
it is true we hold the world intact and
without us it would implode, my body
your heart, I finally know what it means
to roll all time up into one ball, when I
think of you I see you in that black hat
with the black veil, I tell you not to move
you are eternal then, you don't even blink

denmark

where will the king be when the kingdom arrives
no one cares, it's the queen always, the queen coming
the queen's hair like a sacred heart the queen's hair
piled like a hive and her flowing sleeves as wide as doorways,
her soul is pure and loving, even her cruelties are a kind of love
you and I are not the queen, the queen must die
you and I have too many things left to do

and sex, no one sees the queen naked except
her thousands of lovers, she leaves their lives
spent and twisted, you think they'd be grateful
for the doorways they sleep in, for the trolleys
that carry them away stacked like dominoes

sundays I still walk to the church, our church although
neither of us has ever been inside, I stand across the plaza
and watch the men and women file out after mass
you can tell who is saved who is damned who must spend
eternity minus one day in purgatory before rising
to harps and singing and all the relatives or maybe none

last sunday when the plaza emptied cold wind and
the sky like a dead man in new clothes the two pilgrims
walked out, they were not from here, maybe denmark
or some other place where there is butter, her hair the girl
a red coat, yes her butter hair a small book in her right hand
the boy a boy but almost a man his hair was thinning maybe
they were married you could see in a minute a god was involved

that's how we talk about it, the look on her face, she knew
every step she took was more necessary than the empire more
than the burdens of our corporate state, how she felt our trials,
maybe she was the chosen messenger but there was no disguise
like your disguise or mine, the wind caught her hair, she brushed
it back from her face without a thought, this is what I have
been trying to say, you always said the gods graced a woman
by gifting her with wonderful breasts, but that is just you, anyone
who sees straight knows a girl is chosen by how she touches her hai

quilts

my mother's mother was elena, she dwelled in the house
of the lord in lisbon upstairs, I saw my mother tend to her
my mother only believed in my father then, she wrapped
elena's beads along her wrist, she was already straw
sunlight bumped against the window the rosaries
gleamed like wasps, we watched her little chest
go up and down I don't know what she was staring at

your nose reminds me of a roman soldier in the pictures
your eyes are like what people say about snow
there is a little beast inside all of us gnawing at the doors
that's what brave is if you ever wondered, it dreams
to glide out over the alleys and streets high like a roof
but in the end it just gives up, there is no amnesty about it

the stairs don't always creak, I want them to creak when
I carry bags of vegetables, fruit, cans, meat, everything, also as
an alarm if the fanatic iron boots try stealing up, you never know
we have become lucky again, we never understand each other
just the little pieces, we are not true about the rest, when the rain
was here we huddled close under the quilts, I would have eaten
the heat coming off your body but I don't know how that works

diamond

these convictions you say you have, you hold
them like you are holding the handle of a shovel
I can't even get out the door anymore, the sun
is like syrup sweating down on everything green
but all I want is a quiet place to dream that I am
someone else, I closed the curtains I swept away
all the pamphlets and put the olivetti on the stovetop

this is how it is for you though you would never say it
it is how it is with me, I see the one thing I want
from you and that kind of desire, it's like banging
against a diamond to make the little rainbows brighter
that means I have to turn my face from everything else
the whole of you is too much, who could accept all that
and what would be the reason anyway, I can't think

when we looked down into the trench where the men
were being so careful uncovering the ruins, they wore
boots like the sheep farmers wear, mud down there
and the brindled stone you could tell remembered its
whiteness, it was humiliated, how did all that marble
get buried there anyway, are people crazy, one man
smoked a pipe and carried a big notebook folded
into the top of his boot, he kept wiping his hands
on his pants he said julius caesar personally enslaved
a million people, why did you look at me when he said that

69.035

Considering the increase in acts against morals in parks and forested areas the police shall establish permanent surveillance. Article 48 of ministerial order 69.035 establishes the following fines for offenders:

1.—hand in hand..............................2$50
2.—hand on it.................................15$00
3.—it in the hand............................30$00
4.—it in it......................................50$00
5.—it behind it...............................100$00
6.—with the tongue on it.................150$00

steerage

when the woman downstairs sings she is always sharp
except when she sings in c, I think the words are russian
sometimes I lie with my ear on the floorboards I muffle
the olivetti though the flat is safe no one will inform
I never walk with shoes, I am silent at night, I am not
your dark lady of the sonnets don't call me that again
what would that make you, your grammar is not that good
you are always saying america america, all your americas
are laid away in books, go ahead board your grand ship
I'm the fugitive here I am weary of your maritime odes
you can sleep in steerage down below with all the noise

I can quiet my heart and it is peace or else it is terror
it has nothing to do with police or edicts, just an emptiness
I can wait all day for the courier to come there is always
new work for me or nothing at all, sometimes I take
the buses to the ferry, they load the autos then the soldiers,
do they go on to holland then or france, I don't want to know
I just want the question in my mind rolling over and over
there is a small pleasure in that, do they never come back

ophelia

because your face is expensive
because you throat is extravagant
because your spiked boots do not hold water
because for years you walked on the skin of the rivers
because there is artifice in your blood, and guile
because there is nothing terrible that I will not say or do
because my heart is good despite
because I can never know behind the curtains or the hand

lie or be mute, is that your geography
for I lie by instinct, I suffer too many compulsions
for in the café-restaurant in the rossio a girl
in a green army cap her hair the wild guinea-bissau
her fingernails scarlet she holds her cup to a silent kiss
because the smell of coffee roasting I cannot find her scent
because one wayward curl cascades a black river down her cheek
because my breast tightens in the breath of her breath
because I light her cigarette and she says her name, ophelia

because she is the one who will banish all wars forever in delirium

for I mean yours, for I mean even mine

lime

you said to tie your hands, I used the red scarf
you said to tie your feet, I used the yellow bandana,
now what I said, just look at me you said
I went back to the kitchen to tend something on the stove

I think the sun was coming up, the gray with the pink
you could see sleep running off like rainwater
I kept the hair under my arms, you said it was
like going home your face and your breath there

the pencils you gave me smell like incense, when
I sharpen them, I use a knife, they are from
paris so they have no erasers, sometimes
on the roof the sun warms my shoulders,

everyone lies because the truth is always worse
the whole flat smells like lime and candle wax, my reports,
my copies are another labor in themselves, I count
them on the bed like they were my own children

aphrodisia

today I typed from the new portuguese letters three pages, *peace,*
the walls of the castle are breached mariana takes pleasure with her body
I will put twenty copies into a hand and then nineteen hands
from there, reports of the trial are everywhere, our three marias,
a comrade comes delivers carbon paper and ribbons she is vapor
in a long coat, no names no words when she leaves she is smoke

I survive on creed and magic, small is invisible, anonymous
has no body, into the kitchens of the motherland quiet truth
hand to hand voice to voice, think of the paper worn to rags
my head is about three seconds to the left of caetano fictions
I keep a quilt under the olivetti, the machine speaks soft
its oil is aphrodisia, sometimes I become too many people
then I rely on gravity or the eyes of a beloved any beloved

wherever you are, it's a crime not to love, love resists,
all the girls are young now, you hear them laughing
it takes nothing to make them laugh, they are washing
themselves clean in the rivers of sex, so did you and I,
when I walk the street with my coat full of bulletins
I know I slow the clocks I know the street rumbles for me
if anyone notices me they snap their eyes away they click

ophelia brought red wine and a pack of gitanas
I slept with her, it made me feel crazy and then tired
we argued, do you think fucking is always political,
it is a conundrum until you really look at the edicts

the prohibitions, when the government goes after
fucking it is always a cover for burying a woman

and you, are you never confused unsure of where
to put your feet, how to breathe, float above these poisons
do you ever wish to escape your life entire, become an other
no, anaktoria, I know you don't I have counted your curses
but also your fortune, your skin has always fit you like skin

absinthe

you should be whatever I want
you should wear lilacs in your hair
you should carry a knife in your pants
you should sing opera and drink absinthe
this is all just for instance, I don't deny
you have a will of your own it's just
that it's not my will, you'll feel the same
no lilacs no absinthe no altars one song

white candle white lily, egg shell by the door
doff a white robe it's naked you I adore
I can do this forever darling rhyme like before
ride on your shoulders love you down on the floor
until one of us slips then we'll do it no more

word

my truest ardor is all danger and ecstatic, it means
that nothing is remanded, the way violence isn't

yes a kiss can be delicate but not for long
here is a violence, I gave ophelia one of your dresses
from that cardboard trunk that's in the cellar now
purple violet that one, it smelled damp
but not in the way you like it, we sewed it
so it fits, when she wears it she laughs, ophelia

no one is young anymore except the young
death is like a plotline in a book, there are only
the various twists, someone could catalogue
them it would become an oracle, you and I
were immortal and now we are not
do you mind very much, the days gallop

we promise ourselves too much, we don't have
any right to, I could have been a bedouin, endless
sand and robes flowing but I am not complete
you do not complete me, I return the favor,
more reports to france england more circulars
more pamphlets more secrets, ophelia knows, she
says to put all the secrets into one word
if you were a word, anaktoria, what would you mean

code

everything you say is coded and veiled said ophelia,
and everything *she* says is coded and veiled, said ophelia
it's the under-language of life in the regime, no matter
how suspect, it is a language that permeates and that
is its safety, it is as much portuguese as it is a look
or which side of the hand you show up or down
or all your english or french or german all of them
it's why you love fucking me so much, she said,
there is no code involved, it is why the government
hates our sex so much, all their laws, it is the cloud

and the sun behind the cloud, the cloud that wishes
to be fog but is not allowed to touch the earth and so
it touches the earth deliberately in fog
do you comprehend me, she said

I knew you before I knew you because you had to exist,
your crazy affliction to love but also your quiet violence
rescripting the books, the news from the streets,
your pamphlets and bulletins, covert rage, garota,
I knew it before I knew it, we are sisters yes
but we are comrades under the skin,
I can tell you now, surely you knew it, I did not meet you
by accident, surely girl you knew and were smart enough
to keep it to yourself, and comrade we eat each other's fire
we hide our light in that same fire, the clock

ticks ticks ticks for everything and all we have to do is listen,
someone's end is always coming and I do not mean death
I mean those little victories of our flesh, you make them word

said ophelia to me

edge

all right where is that edge of doom then
you'd think it was like a cloud bank coming
in off the atlantic gray and tall but I empty
buckets of doom every day too I don't think
you hear much anymore, I am still sleeping
with ophelia, sometimes we ride a ferry out
and buy boxes of cigarettes and bottles
of whisky, the days do not lead everywhere

can you understand why you are awake
and breathing, it doesn't take a hotel to
make you wonder why you belong here
it doesn't take a brand-new kiss but things
conspire, I have learned to enjoy the terror of being
alone alongside the terror of being with someone else
you can go to sleep that way, you'd be surprised

ivory

that woman with the black-cat hair said she loved you,
she did not love you, why did you love to hear
her speak that way

only I love you, only in the face of the world, you,
you are difficult, my own humors are like spools of wire

you're one of those people who never want the storm
to stop screaming, you never want the night to sneak away

it is six minutes after two in the morning, what do you think
I am eating standing by the kitchen sink, the window is open,
I can breathe the river, it tastes like sleep

you have to understand the perfect use of rouge on her lips
in the light in the restaurant, nobody can get through to you

nothing like the sun or the moon either, I carry myself,
no one is going to carry you, sometimes I think I am
a queen, the things I want

don't compare us falsely, I say ivory ivory over and over when
nothing else is moving in the afternoon heat, sometimes
you have to feel your own teeth against your lips

I saw in one of your dreams last night, that woman's eyes,
unreachable land, all I can think of are green valleys and caves
of ice and the simple young in all delight going down to them

the roses can make perfume out of a small breeze, everybody
knows that, just before the sun sets behind the garden I tread
upon the ground, I prick my finger on a thorn, you won't be back

crows

I cannot bear any more these rolling dooms
and epiphanies anaktoria these blue stars
and our names carved into them you know
I can't follow, new york is forfeit, I don't regret,
lisbon is my savior and my light don't ask why
just tremors, I took my temperature today
the sky is full of swallows I call them ravens
or crows, you can be deceived by their advantages
but don't you think they lead horrid lives,
just flying in the air doesn't make anything right

ophelia in the rain says she never cries
you look at her and you believe it
you couldn't cut her with a dagger
I see her breakage but there's no way
to measure it, what would be the point

if I go to ask that woman with the book
of saint cyprian and all the candles,
you win, the prize is worthless though,
you know that already, the tide is coming
up the river so mineral, so opaque, jugs
of oil on the old triremes of the levant,
you know your world has always been peril
I don't know anymore who will throw you a rope

cravos

*thousands of people in the streets and the flower
vendors flush with spring, the crowds handed out
carnations to the rebel soldiers who stuck them in
their gun barrels*

aphrodite

in new york we had the two rivers
you and I were strangers in rags
that city would kill you if you didn't
watch yourself, we watched each other
when I had to run you didn't hesitate
the leaves in the park were falling

I am terrified anaktoria memory is
a false friend and the bearer of all griefs
I have heard others never carry their past
with them so everything becomes new
they celebrate some whispered compact
we know nothing about but then aeneas
carrying old anchises on his back, so where
did aphrodite go off to, I don't forget these things

how will you fail at life, how will I, can you
imagine falling on a sword, and then what
how will you know if your joys were accurate
how will you concede your walls and lands
to the next wave suddenly charging
out of the trees with blood on their teeth

you always said I made too much of small things
but I made much of you, ophelia is a mayfly
in the month of april, I can't stand how you
and she will not last forever, how the empires
will come and go and not a breath wasted on us,

don't be alone, it's a mistake, your trunk
in the cellar, your collar on the doorknob
why do you think there is never enough for you
what are we that we can never lay our heads down

doves

all I want to do is sleep
my body is covered with books like scales
I am too dry to be a fish
I grew up on shakespeare and camões

I can't truly say I had lovers, they were not
lovers, they were like roomers that stayed
a while in summer and you brought them
each morning a white ewer and bowl

you were so hard to fathom because
there was nothing inside you but the
wool of your sorrows, which you would
never let go of because without it
you think you are nothing

have you noticed that all the news
is like water when it should be blood
why haven't you noticed that
what do you see through without me

I like that I don't ever see you on the street
I don't know where you are and that means
I can imagine you stalking the alien
lands of the earth, dressed in blue and green
talking with strangers, still wondering

the cat is at the door, the cat who
lives on the rooftops, she eats the doves,
I have a can of sardines, she is at the door
all I want to do is sleep, her eyes resemble
my eyes, sometimes it's lucky that I don't see you

cough

ophelia is the queen of wands
the girl of the ecstatic pagan kiss and more

I think she has killed before
the valley of a small scar
cups my fingertip
it is beautiful enough that I dare to say so

she is the wild hidden thing in the conjurer's sleeve
I have been tropicalized she says
she smiles but her lips do not part her mouth widens

somewhere inside her there is a shortened laugh
like a cough that you can't really hear

dear god my cheek against the swale of her belly

telephone

take heart the pleiades haven't gone anywhere
and neither has the moon, just you and it is strange
I have to crane my neck to see the sky from my window
I talk to you like I owned a black telephone on the wall
nothing is torn from me, don't worry I don't know why
you linger, you have wilted into words or thoughts this
is important somehow, how can anyone tell where
anyone is or what, just watch how the gulls avoid this

ophelia lies on the couch alone until she lies in bed with me
I read all the time, I copy the bulletins, I eat I make soup
I make love, plus ça change plus ça la meme chose

I came back from the dead once, perdition isn't
so difficult to manage, ophelia says that's just talking
about every morning for her, you never hear angola,
a zigzagged ghost of old stitches runs aslant one buttock
I trace it with my lips too often, she doesn't mind,
she calls it her colonial railroad, but all her emblems
seem so easy for her, I study her ways but of course
she will be the only one who can see past tomorrow

horses

I can remember when I first saw that everything
is contingent on *if,* you were not there yet, *if* launches
everything my love, like the romans catapulting pitch
over doomed walls or the wand that swept across
the night sky and lavished it with cream and lace
if you were not here with whom would I pour ash
on my head and rend my cloth, who would eat my flesh
and drink my breath in all those louche banned ecstasies
how would we get down any street if one eye wasn't closed

so we can deliver ourselves and look out the window
there are people outside who have never owned wallets
the man at the excavation said there were tiny horses
buried all over, maybe they were badges of a secret order,
ophelia today near the campo, two soldiers fought over her
sujo from guinea, lucky boy soldier to get punched
by lucky boy soldier, what if ophelia had cut him,
then what, she can be like a hot wire herself, yes

and now she is soldering the radio back together
she pulls the long iron from the stove burner
and drops molten beads, I thought of sex and then tears
we are going to listen to music together girl, she says,
every night no matter what, jose vasconcelos limite
we don't ever plant a flag coitada, we just stay clean
there's already enough blood for everybody's hands

cavalry

you are safe with me coitada says ophelia
and I am safe with you, you are beyond repeal,
your french pamphlets your little newspapers

I don't know where she goes when she goes
it's work she says, I can't tell what's going on,
are you a spy I said, no she said I am the cavalry

anaktoria do you see how love divides and steals
ophelia is capable of anything, she walks through
the desert she hides in the jungle she screams in bed
I use a pillow, she holds it in her mouth she thrashes
this is freedom garota she says after, do I scare you

freedom her brow beads of sweat tiny dark pearls
she misunderstands, she doesn't scare me at all

grândola

I found a chain and crucifix of *Aljustrel* silver
I won't tell you where or how it became mine
every day now the waiting, something starves in me
nights when ophelia is gone I rise like a vine on a stake
all my tremors behave like foreign currency

I still think of you too much, we did so much harm
to everything even the clocks even the mice in the cellar
which you insisted were rats, they were, don't presume,
I have always talked to people who aren't here

anaktoria, today in the park two boys and two girls
I lay on the grass abreast of the peonies
they had a guitar they were singing
you could only guess at who was the lover of whom

singing and people had stopped on the walk
the pretty girls and their boys got careless
that's when the three men jumped
from a bench and ran over, not that song
it is not permitted they had been waiting for it

they slapped the girls they kicked the boys
and then one of them stepped all over the guitar
a fool with his feet catching in the splinters
and strings, they squalled and twanged

I was up I was screaming leave them alone

no one on the walk did anything the men
never looked at me they kept punching
shoving the kids, they played the wrong song
forbidden, communists whores faggots

one of the girls, blood in her mouth, spit a tooth
into one of their faces and they ran away singing
that song again grândola the little crowd cheered
the men strutted they thought it was for themselves

braille

if you want to recuperate the morning will never oblige you,
all that murk in your earnest blood and disorder pressing
in the dark, isn't that what we agreed on when you heard
the bells pealing from the church towers even though
they were silent, you can't touch the thing that makes
you yourself, not when there is any light playing over it,
put out your hand and touch a late shadow, lean on that,
it is a friend if you are lucky, I don't say this to hurt you

ophelia watches me with her long eyes, sometimes I forget
too much, I want to hide my name in a word, words are
just air in a mouth she says, I swing the cleaver I split
the chicken and lay it in the pot, show me one truth she
says, she will not stay with me long that's not on anyone's
map, I touched her all over, there is some secret braille
in her skin, I wept like jesus, there is too much to ever
reach for in our breathless city, if something came to ravage
us all wouldn't you batter down the gates to meet it too

bread

no ophelia is not something I have created
you have to pull yourself together, that
implies parts spread out or left behind
are you scattered strewn like wreckage

ophelia's kisses sometimes taste like vodka
they don't ever make me think of you

you're one of the rescriptors ophelia said when
she first saw the boxes and papers the olivetti,
I didn't know they came in red she said,
the free press, she said, I like a girl with patience

she brings recordings and a phonograph we
drink whisky and listen to old fado and coltrane
the stones, I don't know where she gets these things,
I used to be the one with the secrets, anaktoria
I believe I am supposed to love her, it's so strange

everyone I have ever loved has been a great mistake
on both sides, you'd think a person might learn, I told
her this, our legs tangle we sleep into our own oblivions
she drinks coffee in the mornings she scolds me when
I confuse love with ideas, she burns st. jude candles
she fries bread in eggs, I just don't know about her,
so who will close your eyes when you die she says

what

ophelia with the silver cross between her breasts
that sugar and coffee skin the tropic of her body
her mind singing, she cannot be understood in
the way that you can, you can never see her intention
until it moves toward something in the cluttered room
this is not to say that the world is not her property
but its measure ranges inside her, you read it but only
the way you read a cloud for instance and understand
how it occults rain or thunder or a hidden moon glowing

because I am condemned to love I find absurd things
in all the closets of my head, I should learn restraint
I should bring my mouth to heel, we will never stop
having what we had, you and I, that is something
that was settled by the forces of the stars, I found
your natal chart among some things, I don't
mean those stars, when ophelia works at the table her
back is erect her secret books make a palisade in front of her
she is a girl who can travel great distances in thought
I told her everything about us why I came back
and with you, and she believes our hearts were pure,
when she feels my gaze she looks at me, what, she says

war

you are not melancholic if the humors
that force you down, not paranoiac
if the police truly watch you
it is correct to escape into any form
you can manage sometimes
just breathing is resistance

yes said ophelia
but don't speak too much about heroics
maybe your own struggle with who you are
isn't grand enough, you have to tether it
to a war with the regime, all your dangers
are flirtations, I know they keep you here
you like your moldy comfort

and you, ophelia, what about your own moldy comfort
you knew what was going to happen from the beginning
and what am I supposed to do differently

she brushed my cheek
not a thing, type your hopeful subversions whatever,
they change the world as much
as any army ever will

it's truth, writing and copying don't kill anyone I said

her eyes didn't move her face didn't move
you think nothing ever gets into her she

holds herself like a statue apart from everything
well I guess you have pulled ahead then, she said

notas

without us rising they entered the city with their tanks and their guns
the hidden ruins wept for the lost empires under the earth of lisbon

what is this sorrow like a lover drawing far away and no reason
myrrh and cassia and incense rode on the wind

the carnations had been harvested the square was blotched with red
it was a song past midnight all the streets rumbled for grândola

25 de abril sempre
flags flags thickets gardens orchards

a woman sat against a building weeping and trembling the crowd sa
the smell of our bodies hands clapping time, liberate the marias

all our work and secrets and then the army we never knew
it is true a soul comes in three parts they do not always agree

the captains the soldiers killed no one the flowers in gun barrels
I cannot find ophelia all the men in their jungle caps and helmets

we could hardly walk the crush of bodies we could not fall so thick
dancing till night a fire in the alley caetano is gone he's taken away

the man who taps me points look at them nobody is thinking what's n
when my mind is like a wire leading nowhere

still nobody has seen rosa oh anaktoria you are on a shelf far away
or is someone chanting turn on the lights turn on the lights

do not think again about living near to the wild heart
if you approach the wild heart run from it but of course you cannot

este caderno é propriedade de renata elena ferreira
one more note we cannot see the sky from here

armor

the girls my love how they looked at the soldiers
and the soldiers bewildered did they expect to
come shooting those long guns the noise never
stopped the shouts the songs don't you know
my world was swept away in a carpet of
spring flowers now my heart was a hammer

and don't you know that hammers always break
themselves on their anvils for trying so hard
to be hard, I don't know why I was weeping
you were not there ophelia had disappeared among
the treads and armor of course she knew of course
she could not tell me, I had already been questioned
she kept me safe I love her resolute and able

girls and women pushed to kiss a tank
I joined I pressed I kissed the iron skin not cold
but warm something rumbling within and
two men's heads sticking up from hatches
and laughing and blowing kisses back the air
trembled you could see everyone wanted to
be in everyone else's bodies you could tell
nothing could go on like this there would be
shells and husks and ruins collisions the gods
were among the people, you couldn't judge whose
eyes they hid behind never a good sign but maybe
the dark little girl, smudges on her face bare feet
she was staring from nowhere and waving a flag

books

I gathered carnations all I could hold
and took them home I pressed them in books
you don't have to guess which ones, the blossoms
will become fossil or antique but anaktoria they
transform the pages, also you can feel that embrace
in your own nerves, there is the clever smell of passage
in the rooms, you breathe it, it lets you widen your eyes

crocuses

It is true my companheira I am a fugitive you
erred in throwing that at me and that I stay
here because in lisbon everyone is fugitive
I don't need that kind of kinship, I live here in
my heart, that word again, is there no other
way to say that thing that rules me

ruy belo says his only country is where he feels at home
it's where he pays for that feeling with suffering
I should only speak for myself when the electricity
stutters and has its fits, I light candles, when the
ice wagon rolls empty everything is simply warm

I have good papers I can go anywhere except back
you can go anywhere and you do but now you
understand you have a different life here inside me
ophelia tries to say I only invented you or perhaps
you are some sort of lint in my brain's pocketbook
I have almost convinced her it doesn't matter

do you feel constricted then, do you feel this tug
of another life running like a dynamo someplace
and you don't know what that means, I'm saying
when you sense that lightning hum it is me your
beginning and your neverending, I think in new
york now the crocuses are rising, I think you might
need a brighter scarf and white slippers like ballet

trust me anaktoria, if ophelia is right
you'll see you already have them

tired

what made you so tired

when the unions marched in my mother's time
the poets memorized their lines so there were no words
on paper for salazar's police

why were you wringing your hands

what were you trying to tell me, you say it's nothing, our work
we didn't know the cavalry would roll no one did

ophelia knew

who then is making the rain hammer like someone typing on the ro

where is our generalíssimo now, what can he proclaim in his novena

where were you when we owned the streets and our songs
and all the red carnations onto the rooftops and into the gutters

what was it that struck us invisible the revolution we had no idea
where were you when we made that fire in the moonlight who
were you when everybody talked about hearts and sorrows

why were you tired, people are laughing everywhere,
there will be weddings, green wine is sitting on the shelf

what made you so weary when the cravos were budding in their furrow

what made you sit and sit on the stone wall of the white church
with no sermons and no wit, where have the hummingbirds gone

when the singing in the alley near the largo do carmo went
on and on, when the women sweating, when the young girls
wearing razors in their eyes

how does the noise of the horrors of the world always turn
into music no matter whose heart or how much trouble

What is it you were trying to tell me with your hair and your fingers,
I never knew, something about the daylight, something
outside the window, I never knew, why were you so tired

eleven

ophelia I can name you and conjure you from the busy street
anaktoria I can name but the grammar is slipping away
you are ophelia and the other is turning into a ghost
in the overhead wires, she must not become long distance ringing
you are not complete in my heart yet, I am not in yours
we are spinning this way like sufis in white gowns, we must move

yes we are going, we are going, it is ordained
that we push a skiff into the tide the tide takes us up
as it rises, there are eleven gulls on the water
each one is named ophelia, the boat is named ophelia
I have tasted your kiss since this morning I will never
wash, there is a baptism, you and I know sin is a lie

you must never tear open your own breast,
someone else always does that for you then everything
floods in, we have to be careful ophelia, we don't want
to fall in love with our old torments, that will lead us
nowhere, you don't have to ask me how I know, I know

reach

but listen, camões is still singing, *see o nymphs what*
clear vision your tagus nurtures in its worthies,
so come then anaktoria, it's enough, come with me, come
with ophelia we always knew there would be room

we are dipping our oars in the brackish reach of our river
the water is like polish on the barrel of a gun or the eye
behind a violent kiss, when we row the water skids
from the blades of the oars and drops opals in the sun
but only between our heartbeats, the naked ocean waits,
it is luster and bliss, there is a horizon but it is so far away
we cannot see it, we are making way and you too anaktoria

come and sit among the ropes and winches you were
always the one with the sail, ophelia holds the dagger, I carry
the one direction which is not a star, florbela said
I love and I love and I love, are we all not in accord
we are broken from love and that's how we became one another

let the empires fade or blaze behind us, I don't know what
we will ever claim for our own but this won't be the epic voyage
surely no dream for a shining new world

you know as much as I do there was never any such thing

NOTES TO FOREWORD

PAGE 3

In the foreword I note that the summer visitors and the Portuguese families in the West End of Provincetown, circa 1955–65, formed a close and congenial hybrid community. Contrast that description with what the *New Yorker* had to say about the Provincetown Portuguese in the June 9, 1986, issue (p. 88). The tone in observing the implicitly inferior "other" continues a pervasive and clichéd denigration of the Portuguese that goes back at least to Herman Melville's essay, "The 'Gees." The following anecdote about the woman becoming lost in the tiny neighborhood is typical of the "humor" that appears in much of such writing about Portuguese Americans.

The Portuguese of the purest blood have black hair and dark eyes and dark skin. To the summer community they are aloof and all but invisible. They stay home. They live back from the main part of town, in a neighborhood of newer houses, at the center of which is the Catholic Church, and, except for the amusement of watching the summer crowds, they generally avoid the congestion of traffic downtown. They trim their hedges and water their lawns and watch television. They are not especially given to curiosity. The mother of one of the fishermen lived twenty-one years in the West End of town and recently moved a mile or so away to the East End. On her first day out shopping, she became lost, and had to call someone to take her home.

PAGE 4

velhos, velhas

the old men and women

saudades

Saudade is the name of a complex of emotions, some of them seemingly contradictory. It is often characterized as being untranslatable, but that may merely mean there is no strict cognate in English. Yet the feelings and thoughts inherent in the term seem to me universal. They are certainly not the exclusive property of some imagined Latin temperament of the Portuguese. I know that I felt *saudade* long before I ever heard the word. And if a definition is vexed, a description might offer a small light. It is a dreaminess that is not listless, a kind of breathing when the heart settles on something that is absent but not lost, for the nexus of emotion itself keeps the object present. In fact, it is tempting to say that in *saudade* there is a melding of subject and object. In English, for instance, when we say *longing*, the word *long* is encapsulated, and we understand desire for something at a distance, real or psychic, a desire for something not present, something we do not have (the Latinate origins of *desire* say something like "your star is down," a bummer if I've ever heard one). But the feeling of *saudade*, which can be almost trance-like if we indulge it, is a conjuring, a *making-present* in the memory, even as the object cannot be touched. I believe that when Ana Bento's grandmother (p. 35) refuses to curtail her diet as treatment for her blood pressure, saying, "When I die, I am going to die with my belly full," *saudade* is present as an aggregate of hunger, the hardscrabble living on the island of her birth, heating water over kerosene, a small unlighted cottage, hard work, the cold Atlantic winds in winter; but also the warmth of bodies in the home, the smell of soup simmering long, the green fields, the smells of her own mother when she held her, the sound of the bed when her tired husband slipped in late beside her. And all this in the context of the comforts of America (which she will not refuse), the happiness of the extended family now around her, the unburdened ease of living, heat in winter, the abundance of the kitchen table: the memory and the present, together, combining feelings and sensations that do not agree with each other, except that in *saudade*, they do. It may be that the word (a lush, pretty word, to my ear) is floating among the sugars of poetry rather than sitting in the mousetrap of analysis. I would submit that in its poetry resides its power. This is all insufficient, of course. But the beauty of that word and all it contains can't be gainsaid. I think of all those feelings, vivid, living in all of us, each to his or her own. They are there, I believe, and not strange or alien in any way. *Saudade.*

PAGE 6

The Cold Storage, built in 1905, was a major place of employment for men and women in the neighborhood around it. Its structure, along with outbuildings, all in bad repair, were torn down in 1975. During the sixties, the old-timers liked to say that the only thing keeping the main building from falling down was the ice in the freezers. A narrow wharf extended from the plant out into deeper water, where boats unloaded their catch. The fish would then be hauled up to the main building by tram. The twisted pilings of the old wharf can still be seen today at low tide.

PAGE 9

We looked at a show of Renata's in one of the East End galleries. There were boxes of all sizes, and objects inside them, framed by them. The boxes themselves were covered in designs of heavy bright paint. In a draft of an unfinished poem that she did not include in the designated manuscript Renata mentions the artist Hélio Oiticica (1937–80), the Brazilian modernist best known for his boxes (*bólides*) and environmental spaces (*parangolés*), but who also worked in other media. She says in a note among the few other papers included in the typewriter box that she "knew Hélio in Brazil," likely in Rio de Janeiro, but there is no corroboration of this. Neither do their times in New York seem to have coincided. Nonetheless, he may have influenced her construction pieces.

A "weasel" is a short, wide-beamed sailboat, heavy, with the mast stepped up near the bow. Easy to sail, they were once plentiful in the harbor.

PAGE 10

He told me how he had been drafted and had to report to the draft facility. . . . He was talking about Vietnam

The Tonkin Gulf Resolution had been passed on August 7, 1964, the summer before I talked with Santos de Melo. It essentially gave President Johnson authority to escalate the war effort in Vietnam. Americans were feeling the results of this action, and it became a divisive issue almost immediately. There was no draft lottery system at this time (the lottery did not go into effect until December 1969), and anyone with a draft card could be called up at any time without warning. Most draftees were drawn from the working classes. College students were then exempt, and elaborate schemes were concocted by the more privileged classes to avoid conscription. These included spurious medical excuses from family physicians, or claims of financial hardship, equally spurious. I do not have the exact date, but sometime in the late seventies, back on the Cape, Santos de Melo shot himself with a .22 rifle, the stock of which he had sawn off to accommodate the barrel's position against his throat.

PAGE 11

Miss de Beers was well-read and conversant in the arts and music. She laced her conversations and monologues with bits and pieces—phrases—from many sources, some of which I could catch right away. At that time, though, I would have missed most of them. It wasn't a game with her, I later learned. She just talked that way. I would come to realize that her personality had many facets. She was polished and sophisticated, she could be both sincere and disingenuous, she was imperious and yet seductive. I make these judgments long after the year that I knew her.

PAGE 12

West Thirtieth Street was then a tough and rundown but relatively safe neighborhood, hardly the gentrified Chelsea of today. A vacant lot lay next to our building, and the building just east of the lot was a shambling brothel where some of the girls would sit on the stoop and jive and joke with us. Ronnie and Rainey sometimes played and sang with them. We often ate around the corner on Tenth Avenue at a little diner run by two men, Michael and Floyd. Floyd was missing a front tooth. He claimed to have once run stolen cars for the mob. Seventy-five cents bought a bowl of soup and four slices of toast. There was a row in front of the brothel once (it was called the Sun Hotel)—a guy was threatening one of the girls. Dexter and I were going to jump in, but then Mr. Franks, a large man with iridescent black skin and a glass eye, walked calmly out the door with a revolver and things settled down very quickly. The gun was probably a .38, but it seems like a cannon in memory. Mr. Franks owned the Sun Hotel. He liked us. He could play guitar, too. He was always natty, in a suit and tie. He could have been a banker. This was a different time. We all felt very much at home on those streets.

A note upon the above note is deserved: Mr. Franks owned a vintage f-hole guitar and could play slide with the blunt edge of a straight razor. He fought in Patton's Army, light armor, the 176 Black Panthers, the only all African American unit in Europe. The 176 broke through the Battle of the Bulge, fighting against German heavier armor and outmaneuvering them. It was in this battle that Mr. Franks lost his eye. In the right mood he would tell us the stories. He was highly decorated along with the entire unit. The war in Vietnam disgusted him.

PAGE 17

In September of that year, the United States deployed its first army combat division to Vietnam. (The marines and the navy were already there.) America was now engaged directly in military operations, and troop levels had increased to more than 200,000. The number would reach 400,000 in a matter of months. Industries involved in support and supply for the war effort found lucrative opportunities during this time, and Hammond Marine was among them.

PAGE 19

Far Rockaway

Far Rockaway is a seaside neighborhood in Queens, considered rough but not dangerous then. It was at that time the terminus of the BMT Subway line—"the end of the road." Renata's meaning was clearly ironic, and perhaps cautionary, but nothing in my notebooks shows any speculation or reflection on my part. I did scrawl a note that I thought the name "sounded cool."

PAGE 26

Even though we shared the writing space, I never saw any draft or other evidence of this project (and I would never have gone hunting for it if it had been stashed away someplace). But Renata did crew for a week or so with Joaquim Dutra sometime in the early sixties, when his brother Bobbie, who ran the dragger with him, was laid up sick. It was my guess that the experience might have given her the idea for the play. But the story that went around the neighborhood back then was that, when it was time to settle up shares at Joaquim's kitchen table, Renata wouldn't take any money. She demanded payment in fish boxes. True or not, this became a great joke between the two of them and around the neighborhood as well.

Dragger is another name for trawler, in Provincetown usually a boat between about forty and eighty feet in length, with a beam of about fifteen feet (there are much larger trawlers in other Massachusetts ports, such as New Bedford and Gloucester). These boats pull a large net, or trawl, to capture fish.

PAGE 28

The whole city was dark, and a huge moon was just rising over the buildings toward the east.

This was the beginning of the major blackout that covered eight states in the Northeast. There was a large amount of confusion about this at first. The idea that we had been attacked by the Soviet Union carried a great deal of credence, civil defense responders were called out, and air traffic, among other major activities, was halted along the East Coast. Once the magnitude of the blackout became known, speculation spread. The power remained out until about six the next morning. The cause was eventually traced to an equipment malfunction.

PAGE 28

A Catholic Worker who burned himself

On November 9, Roger Allen Laport, a member of the Catholic Workers, burned himself in front of the United Nations building in protest against the Vietnam War. A week before, on November 2, Norman Morrison, a Quaker, set himself on fire in protest at the Pentagon under the window of Robert McNamara, the U.S. Secretary of Defense.

Buddhist monks

On June 23, 1963, Thich Quang Duc immolated himself on a street in Saigon to protest the religious oppression by the Vietnamese government. This action was captured on film and was circulated widely. Five other monks followed him over a period of time.

PAGE 30
attack on Salazar's personal character

Salazar was often lampooned in underground circles, but the "attack on character" here might have to do with his double life. An unmarried man who presented a chaste exterior and preached a harsh morality, he was rumored to have had several mistresses, and had been seen and photographed in their company despite efforts to keep his indiscretions secret. Any piece of writing mocking Salazar's behavior would provoke outrage and retaliation, and this might have been the extreme nature of the document that Renata's father read that night. This subject has been researched by Felícia Cabrita in her book, *Os Amores de Salazar*, among other sources.

PAGE 31

It is not possible to find complete or reliable records of detainment at Tarrafal during this period. In any case, the story may have morphed over a number of repetitions. Tarrafal was distant, and there were several other centers for interrogation, imprisonment, and torture right in Lisbon. Accounts are aggravated further by the conflicting versions of Renata's father's role in prerevolutionary times.

PAGE 33
works

Works was one of the commonly used names for the apparatus of injecting heroin. Carrying works was still a crime in New York at that time, and only street junkies would carry them outside. Usually they were crude and makeshift, an eye-dropper fitted with the tip of a hypodermic needle by making a "collar" or gasket out of a thin sliver cut from a dollar bill or some other resilient material. The bulb of the eyedropper was replaced with the nipple from a baby's bottle or pacifier, giving more power to the shot. Renata's works, however, were simply a medical hypodermic needle, kept in a flat rectangular tobacco tin lined with gauze—

always clean. To the top of the tin she had glued a dark and eerie picture of a pretty young girl looking through the knothole in a wrecked and partially burned fence. Wind blowing through her black hair, along with the charring on the fence post, created the illusion of demon-like horns on the girl's head. You understood something terrible had happened. I didn't have to think about what led Renata to choose that image. I could see it in her own face. The cover became iconic; it was the paperback cover of Shirley Jackson's *We Have Always Lived in the Castle*. But it was about knowing terror, and how one cannot really comprehend the terror in the other unless she has experienced terrors of her own. And then you can understand the responses to terror—that there are no limits or frontiers to them. Guile and savagery, for instance. The capability of doing absolutely anything to annihilate its source, or of gaining relief from it, no matter where it took you. And that knowledge opened you to a deep capacity for tolerance and empathy—a grace that allowed you to offer any part of yourself to the terrified, to gentle his or her heart. That was all there in that child's stylized face. The demonic and the compassionate, the fearful and the fierce. All that is already stored inside you someplace waiting to get called up. Renata dug all that, and it jumped to me, too. Now there would come a release. Like so many potent emblems, that picture wasn't high art; it was just a color illustration on a paperback book. But that image, Renata's face, that tin box and its purpose, left their permanent brand on me. I say none of this as complaint.

PAGE 36

Hammond's outburst about Renata's tale of her father, and about Elena's and Renata's flight to America, complicates later speculation as to why Renata chose to live in Salazar's (Caetano's) Lisbon and become part of the resistance to the fascist government. It is not possible to know whether such activity was the motive for her moving there or whether her involvement developed after she had lived there for a time. Certainly her feelings about political activism were evident in New York. Whatever the case, there is no reason to believe that the poems are not an authentic record of her life in Lisbon. Salazar seems to have held a signal place in her psyche, and her father's involvement (either with Salazar or against him) may have bound her to her struggle in profound ways.

PAGE 39

The editor I refer to is Christopher Larkosh, then director of Tagus Press.

PAGE 42

Re the matter of Renata's other effects: the typewriter and the pages inside its box were specifically bequeathed (or in the case of the Underwood, returned) to me. Ana and Rafael Lewis are holding the other materials in trust, until due diligence can declare provenance. Renata would be in her eighties at the time of this writing, and her whereabouts are unknown. I am hopeful that at some point more material will be available for publication or scholarly use. Although I cannot quote from said material, I may state that a good deal of it is in Portuguese as well as English. There are some letters, some pages concerning artworks, some notebooks, and perhaps some poems and other creative pieces. From evidence found within this material, one can infer that some of Renata's Portuguese-language poems were circulated along with rescripted material, and were known to members of the resistance.

PAGE 44

rooted in eros

Renata at times appears to regard the erotic as reaching beyond the flesh to indicate more transcendent states. This idea is put forth in Plato's *Symposium* and in the work of later writers and thinkers, particularly Marsilio Ficino, who glossed and expanded on Plato's thinking during the Renaissance. Renata would have known both of these writers.

PAGE 44

To evade the fascists' heavy censorship, clandestine communications were passed from hand to hand. These were often news items copied from other countries' journals, or from other banned sources. Also, bulletins containing otherwise suppressed news of events and conditions within Portugal were passed on to European outlets. This system of communication was a holdover from communist underground operations run by women, whose place was "in the home" under *Estado Novo* and who could work undetected on these so-called clandestine typographies. Cristina Marques Nogueira, writing in the *Journal of Social Science Education* (2015, vol. 14, no. 2) gives accounts of "typographies" as well as other varied activities of communist and resistance underground operations. Renata mentions the resistance and "sisters," but nowhere does she declare any affiliation with the Communist Party, and her rescripting arrangement does not follow the communist model of a man and woman posing as married and living in a house rented specifically for secret activity.

Fragment numbers of Sappho's work appear ordered differently in different translations or compilations. It is not possible to ascertain which translations Renata may have used. I have relied here mainly upon Diane Rayor and André Lardinois in their comprehensive *Sappho* (Cambridge University Press, 2014).

PAGE 51

Salazar defended his continuing colonization of Africa by adopting the term *Lusotropicalism* as put forth in the books and lectures of Gilberto Freyre (1900–1987), a Brazilian social critic and historian. According to Salazar's appropriation of Freyre's thesis, Portugal was bringing about equality of the races as well as setting the stage for cultural exchanges that would foster education and the mutual accrual of experiential knowledge. (In her preface to José Luandino Vieira's *Short*

Stories of Angola, Tamara Bender ironically refers to Lusotropicalism as Portugal's "mythology of a special aptitude for integrating with tropical peoples.") Despite what the dictator was presenting to the world, the stark truth was a rigid colonial rule that resulted in cheap or forced labor, mistreatment of the native populations, poverty, and substandard living conditions. By the 1960s, Mozambique, Angola, and Guinea-Bissau were fighting for their independence. These foreign wars elicited little support and substantial resistance from the Portuguese people.

NOTES TO POEMS

PAGE 53 Epigraphs

Renata opens the collection of poems with two epigraphs, and it is significant that they are each heteronyms of Fernando Pessoa (1888–1935), Portugal's great modernist poet. Pessoa was inhabited by a number of distinct personalities, some of whom were poets whose writing was markedly divergent from his own. Ricardo Reis and Álvaro de Campos are two of his major four (I would include Alberto Caero and Bernardo Soares in this group). Reis is an Epicure, though at times, melancholy; de Campos seems intent on being somewhat scandalous (and he does smoke opium). One might sense vague parameters set by these two, and Renata's not mentioning Pessoa seems to indicate her understanding that a heteronym is indeed a separate entity.

PAGE 55 Epigraph to *"anaktoria"*

From Sappho, fragment no. 1, sometimes referred to as "Hymn to Aphrodite."

PAGE 57 island

The island is presumably Lesbos. Anaktoria is a young girl who has left Sappho's inner circle. (Some commentators speculate that she left to marry.) The poem also references Sappho's wedding hymn 59. J.D. Salinger uses its famous line as the title of a volume containing his two short novellas, *Raise High the Roofbeam, Carpenters* and *Seymour: An Introduction.*

As the phrase "what you wrote in pencil" makes clear, Renata addresses her own lover as Anaktoria here and throughout the collection. She is, however, not the only poet to have written subsequently to an Anaktoria. Algernon Charles Swinburne (1837–1909) portrays the speaker, Sappho, as an inflamed sadist who, in flowing rhyme and meter, describes hideous and prolonged tortures she will inflict upon the young girl, resulting in her death. The long poem has been both derided and praised.

PAGE 59 knot

The third stanza repeats a segment of Renata's tale of how she and her mother fled Portugal. As I mentioned in the foreword, it is not possible to determine exactly which account is more accurate, hers or Hammond's. Renata may be relating the story as it happened, based on her mother's account, which might have been altered by Elena to be more acceptable in America and to the psyche of a young girl. Conversely, although Hammond was not necessarily the more dependable narrator, given his feelings about Renata, his version could still be the correct one. Renata, if she knew that version to be true, could have invented the story that appears in this poem and in the foreword. It may remain an unsettled issue in Renata's biography—that is, what little we have of one.

PAGE 60 swans

See Plato's *Phaedo*, which recounts the death of Socrates. Socrates likened himself to the swans, who sing best when their death is near. The swans, because they serve the god Apollo, are gifted with prophecy, as is Apollo himself. Socrates famously sat composing a hymn to Apollo as he awaited his death by hemlock.

PAGE 61 wedge

The word "cunt" (Port. *cona*) stems from the Latin *cuneus*, 'wedge,' as do many words in English and other languages. The word *cuneiform*, for instance, denotes the form of impressions that make up the "wedge writing" of the Babylonians. Halfway between Turin and Nice there is a town called Cuneo, nestled in a lovely passage between rounded mountains. One cannot but wonder at the medieval imagination.

PAGE 63 bone

Catholic altars all contain a relic, a bone of a saint or martyr.

Scissor as a verb can refer to certain sexual activity.

PAGE 64 peru

rouge . . . horrid book . . . whipped

The poem may be referring to *The Story of O* by Pauline Réage (possibly a pseudonym). The book details the life of a young woman who willingly enters into a life of sexual torture and slavery in the name of love. It was one of the many books banned by the Portuguese government at this time. A random sample from long lists of banned authors includes Alan Payton, Jean-Paul Sartre, Vladimir Nabokov, William Faulkner, Simone de Beauvoir, Mary Wollstonecraft, John Dos Passos, Albert Camus, Leo Tolstoy, Fyodor Dostoevsky, and of course, The Three Marias.

PAGE 66 list

See Shakespeare's sonnet no. 147, "My love is as a fever."

PAGE 67 leather

The poem suggests that Anaktoria was in Renata's presence at the time of the described incident. The references to marine supplies seem in accord with her background, but how and under what auspices is not clear, though Hammond was probably not involved. Her mention of the bulletins demonstrates that she was active in the underground network that served as the free press of the resistance. The poem shows that the exchange of information ran both into and out of Portugal.

The PIDE is not named here, nor the location where the interrogation took place. It is possible that she was briefly held in the notorious prison and torture facility on Rua António Maria Cardoso. We might surmise that because of Renata's dual citizenship (which we must assume, and which would not necessarily have been known at once to the police) nothing further occurred. It is also possible that her maritime work was with friendly international companies and might also have mitigated her circumstances. She did appear to operate with caution but also with a certain measure of impunity.

The Three Marias are Maria Isabel Barreno, Maria Velo da Costa, and Maria Teresa Horta, three young women with substantial literary backgrounds who together wrote a volume of poems, essays, letters, memoirs, fictions, manifestos, and chronicles in the form of a three-way unsigned correspondence. Titled *New Portuguese Letters*, it was published in 1972. The title refers to *Letters of a Portuguese Nun*, the story of a young woman who is seduced and abandoned by her lover while she is in a convent. It was first published sometime in the mid-1600s. *New Portuguese Letters* became a significant treatise on the state of women in Portugal, historically, and particularly during the fascist regime. It is a defiant challenge to repression—erotic, at times graphic, and astutely seditious. The book quickly became an international sensation, especially when The Three Marias, as they were known, were arrested for pornography and indecency and were subjected to a lengthy trial. They were not freed until the 1974 revolution.

This was a brave and dangerous book to write in a climate of suppression when thousands of dissenters faced torture and imprisonment every day. The Marias paid a severe price for having written it. Yet a review in the *New York Times* (February 2, 1975) exhibits little understanding of its cultural and political importance and is notably dismissive:

> [In] their portraits of imagined sisters through the centuries, the convent of Soror Mariana becomes a metaphor for the bedroom,

and the bedroom for the world to which women are confined—which is appropriate, since their women rarely seem to leave their bedrooms except to go mad or kill themselves. But the impression one gets from this is that the women of Portugal are all in a state of torpid but advanced sexual hysteria, or a state of sexual repression which is itself a kind of frozen hysteria. Whatever they may say, it is not the nature of sexual combat that concerns the three Marias; it seems to be the disease itself that attracts them. Their poems and portraits, despite their occasional virtuosity, read like little hymns to fever instead of cool towels on the forehead. Their Marias, in desire or revulsion, exude a kind of southern heat that is passive, stifling and exultant. They parody all the myths of Latin temperament.

PAGE 68 radio

Marcello José das Neves Alves Caetano took power in 1968 after Salazar suffered a debilitating stroke. He enacted certain liberal reforms to the previous Salazar regime, but they seemed ineffective, and he perpetuated the culture of oppression (still using informants) along with continuing the vastly unpopular African colonial wars. He changed the name of the PIDE to the General Directorate of Security, GDS, but the people never stopped using the original name, with its terrifying connotations. He was deposed in the April 25, 1974, Carnation Revolution.

The *Diário de Notícias* was a right-wing newspaper that carried government propaganda and generally conservative-slanted news stories.

Renata would have known the story of Judith and Holofernes from the Catholic Bible (the story does not appear in all versions of the Old Testament) or through art. Holofernes, an enemy general, is readying to attack the Jews with a powerful military force, but a young Jewish woman, Judith, plies him with wine until he is drunk and incapacitated. She then severs his head and averts a certain martial defeat. The tale has been a subject for numerous artists, from Caravaggio to Klimt.

PAGE 73 jump

Renata's mention of a drug here is ambiguous, given her history with drug use when she was younger. Plato used the word *pharmakon,* meaning both medicine and poison. In one plausible reading, given the language in the rest of the stanza, she may be speaking of love in any of its many facets. In any case, drugs threaten systems of order, power, and control, and however ephemeral the effects on the human spirit, they offer at least a semblance of freedom and transcendence.

PAGE 74 *notas*

The two list poems, *notas,* read like raw fragments transcribed from notebooks or journals. Some of the notes provide ancillary information, others seem undeveloped thoughts, still others are borrowings from other texts. I have kept these pages exactly as written and in the same positions as they were found in the manuscript.

avante, stockholm bulletin, luta, frente patriótica de libertação nacional form a list of progressive and antifascist publications from outside Portugal.

over the darkness of the shining roofs the cold light of morning breaks
mist or smoke was it rising from the earth or falling from the sky
These lines seem to meld Pessoa and Sappho in a way that makes a definite attribution impossible.

The mention of the soldier in the Rossio train station or square suggests that he is either fleeing Portugal to avoid the colonial wars, or he has received orders to go.

laipis azul refers to the censors' blue pencil.
purple ink—often carbon copies were used rather than mimeograph, to avoid detection.

let them ignore the enemy within the gate /while they search for another
so far away
These are lines from Camões's *Lusiads*, canto 4, lines 101, 102, spoken
by a "venerable-looking" old man (*O velho de Restelo*), admonishing da
Gama and his men as they embark on their epic voyage. Placed here,
no doubt, to reference the troubles at home in Portugal in the face of
the "enemies" in Africa. Further interpretations might lead to discus-
sions of colonialism, the export of power, the valorization of conquest,
the ultimate results of exploration, and other subjects pertinent to his-
torical and present geopolitical adventure.

Dutch caps and jelly refer to diaphragms and spermicidal ointment.
Members of underground groups purchased and distributed birth
control to poor women in rural areas. Because the state, the Church,
and many husbands disapproved, this activity was carried out careful-
ly and covertly. It is worth noting that a woman's using contraception
without her husband's knowledge was grounds for divorce. António
Pacheco Palha's *Sexuality in the Time of Salazar's Dictatorship* gives
an informative account of the place of women under the fascist
government.

The line "este caderno não pertence a ninguém" translates as "this
notebook does not belong to anybody."

PAGE 77 rosa
The café here is a gathering place for women and is described with
some degree of specificity, notably, only once it is closed (the windows,
the door). It is likely that "Rosa" is not the woman's real name, and the
café (one of many such, for men and women during this time) could
be anywhere in the city.

PAGE 78 scream

Throughout the book Renata seems careful not to pinpoint where she lives. She gives hints at locations that seem to be geographically contradictory, likely as a gesture toward safety if she intended the poems to be distributed, even among trusted friends, lest they fall into the wrong hands.

PAGE 79 Epigraph to "ophelia"

Taken from Hamlet. "You must wear your rue with a difference," may be the important line to Renata, who, if she rues the situation in Lisbon, she wears it as a badge of activism and transgression.

PAGE 81 girls

In 1917 the Virgin Mary appeared to three shepherd children in the village of Fátima. A shrine and basilica have been erected on the site of the visitations, and hundreds of thousands of pilgrims visit the town each year. Streets in the town are lined with scores of shops that sell religious objects and tourist memorabilia. Such shops are also plentiful in Lisbon and other cities.

PAGE 83 wild

The *Confiteor* is Catholic prayer of contrition, "Oh, my God, I am heartily sorry for having offended thee . . ."

PAGE 84 veil

I finally know what it means to roll all time up into one ball
An allusion to Andrew Marvell's "To His Coy Mistress," lines 41–44, and perhaps also to Eliot's own allusion in "The Love Song of J. Alfred Prufrock," lines 90–93. "Veil" is, in Renata's characteristic idiom, a love song.

PAGE 85 denmark

our church although neither of us has ever been inside
The Catholic Church was closely linked with, and on some issues in-
distinguishable in doctrine from, the Estado Novo's brand of fascism.
In this regard, many Portuguese were alienated from the church, their
church, perhaps, but they were not "within" it. Some activists, though
critical of the Church, remained close to it, as did the poet Sophia de Mel-
lo Breyner Andresen, who believed dissent from within was possible.

PAGE 88 diamond

Lisbon is built upon Roman ruins. The prefix Luso- (as in Luso-Ameri-
can) derives from the Roman name for the region, Lusitania.

PAGE 89 edict

A "found poem." Renata copies from the edict precisely the list of fines
for sexual and same-sex activity signed into law by Salazar. He is fa-
mously photographed at the signing. The fines are in escudos, the cur-
rency in Portugal at the time.

PAGE 90 steerage

The title of the poem calls to mind José Rodrigues Miguéis's long
short story, *Gente da Terceira Classe*, translated as *Steerage* by George
Monteiro, and defined as an uncomfortable and denigrating class of
travel far below decks on the steamships of the last century (though
some readers of Rodrigues Miguéis use the term for flying "coach"
on contemporary airlines). Ginsberg, Shakespeare, and Dickinson lurk
among the allusions. Renata watches the soldiers boarding the ferry,
wondering if they are going for good (we are unsure if they are in uni-
form or identified as soldiers because the resistance is helping them
in their desertion).

PAGE 91 ophelia

Renata seems to introduce Ophelia to Anaktoria, an alluring if somewhat mysterious appearance.

PAGE 93 aphrodisia

... peace, the walls of the castle are breached mariana takes pleasure with her body ...

Renata copies out and distributes a particularly erotic passage from *New Portuguese Letters*. In the same poem she announces the beginning of her sexual affair with ophelia.

PAGE 97 code

Feinting departure from her usual method, this poem appears to take its words from the mouth of Ophelia, but Renata tags it as her own transcription in the very last line.

PAGE 99 edge

Edge of doom—Shakespeare again, sonnet no. 116.

PAGE 102 crows

Renata references her flight from New York after her legal troubles (and supposed death, with help, we understand, from the Hammonds). From this poem, it is possible to suppose that the Anaktoria of the poems might be the lover she had been seeing during her final days with Nina de Beers.

lisbon is my savior ...

Perhaps with some irony, perhaps not, Renata alludes to her relationship with the city. Whatever the reason, she finds purpose and even solace among its troubles

book of saint cyprian

A collection of spells, curses, magic, divination, healing, and love remedies dating back in Portugal to the middle ages. Sometimes thought to be used by conjurers, witches, and evil-doers.

PAGE 103 Epigraph to "cravos" (carnations)

In reference to the revolution on April 25, this could have been an account in any newspaper or bulletin.

PAGE 105 aphrodite

Reference to the fall of Troy and perhaps misgivings about her leaving Anaktoria (if indeed she did) for Ophelia. Aphrodite falls in love and has sex with the mortal Anchises. She bears Aeneas, who goes on to found Rome. At the fall of Troy, Aeneas escapes, carrying old Anchises on his back, that is, carrying his past with him.

PAGE 109 cough

ecstatic pagan kiss
Florbela Espanca from "Exaltation."

queen of wands
From the Tarot—usually associated with powerful feminine energy.

I have been tropicalized
Ophelia has been in Africa, but her status is never clear. She may have been part of the native population or she may have been sent there as a soldier or on some other duty. She seems to have had combat experience, but even that is not clear. Neither is her role on April 25. Whatever her secrets, Renata has kept them veiled. Being tropicalized is evidently an ironic reference to her experience there.

PAGE 110 telephone

Pleiades
The moon (Sappho no. 168).

PAGE 111 horses

we are going to listen to music tonight . . .
This line implies that Ophelia knows something about the radio program and its importance. Renata does not have, or does not indicate

that she has, all the information. The signal for the advance on Lisbon will come from this broadcast.

>   *and drink my breath in all those louche banned ecstasies*
>   *how would we get down any street if one eye wasn't closed*

Renata's allusive wordplay again. Louche, meaning disreputable, is derived from the Latin word "luscus," meaning "one eyed" (and in ancient Rome, a slang term for drunk). One also has to think of Camões here, writing and adventuring with his one eye.

PAGE 113 *grândola*

"Grândola, Vila Morena" is name of the forbidden song. Composed by Zeca Afonso, its lyrics speak of a village where freedom and equality thrive. The government was threatened by its sentiment.

PAGE 116 bread

olivetti, red

Renata mentions this machine several times, but never the Underwood. The Olivetti she speaks of could have been a 1940's MP1, but could also refer to the later Olivetti Valentine. If the latter, it would have been relatively new, something Renata might have allowed herself for her cover work as a maritime supply translator and broker. Having a personal attachment to the Underwood, I found myself speculating what its presence here might mean. It is possible that there were never Olivettis, that any mention of them in the poems was a smokescreen (somewhat in the way Renata keeps slightly altering the details of her lodgings) and that everything was done on the Underwood. While this seemed a matter of personal curiosity, I nevertheless felt that it could be a significant detail in further studies, perhaps in identifying heretofore unknown or unattributed work. I should note here that typewriters, particularly manual typewriters, differentiate themselves in many ways beyond make and model. Even machines with the same typeface leave telltale signs, not unlike ballistic traces in the examination of firearms. Keys loosen, type wears down or becomes dirty, and even the touch of the typist can leave a trail. It is not unreasonable that typewriters might be useful in tracing Renata and her work, or at least corroborating other data. Just as this volume of poems was going to the press, I contacted Ana and Rafael Lewis, and we went through a quick look at the remaining papers via Skype. There was much in handwriting in both English and Portuguese, and text on several types of paper in a number of different fonts. Quite a lot of material, but the Lewises reiterated that we not release any of it publicly until the provenance issues were finalized, and I agreed. We then conferred with my literary editor and decided that in the meantime it would be prudent to have the material privately sorted and cataloged by a university archivist proficient with Portuguese and Portuguese-American collections.

PAGE 117 what

natal chart

Renata mentions Anaktoria's natal chart among her effects. Along with the few papers that were included with Renata's manuscript was a natal chart, but it had Renata's name on it. The chart was drawn with apparently professional symbols and numbers. It appears on an 8½ by 11 sheet of paper, identical to the paper used in the manuscript, but folded into fourths. It is hand drawn in pencil, three concentric circles with a border containing the traditional signs of the zodiac. Outside the circles and symbols, in the upper righthand corner, is the date, 21 de Setembro 1933, underneath which is the time, 12:31. Renata's typed name and her handwritten initial are visible beneath the chart. I include this note because the birthdate on the chart does not corroborate with the date that Renata always gave, 1935. There is no explanation for this difference in anything we have seen from her at this point.

PAGE 120 *notas*

> *what is this sorrow like a lover drawing far away and no reason*
> *myrrh and cassia and incense rode on the wind*

A cutup of lines from Sappho.

> *near to the wild heart*

Likely borrowed from the title of the celebrated 1943 novel *Perto do coração selvagem* by Clarice Lispector, Brazilian novelist and chronicler (1920–77), who evidently borrowed it herself from James Joyce.

The line "este caderno é propriedade de renata elena ferreira" translates as "this notebook is the property of renata elena ferreira."

> *the captains the soldiers killed no one the flowers in gun barrels*

Renata is speaking here of the military takeover by the rebels, who did not create open combat in the city. There were four deaths, however, victims of the PIDE, who fired upon unarmed protesters outside the headquarters at António Maria Cardoso Street. They are commemorated with their names on a plaque which now stands on the facade of the old PIDE headquarters: Fernando C. Gesteira, José J. Barneto, Fernando Barreiros dos Reis, and José Guilherme R. Arruda.

Celeste Martins Caeiro, a woman who worked in a cafe friendly to the resistance, is said to be the first to pass out carnations to the rebel soldiers. Flower sellers immediately followed, filling guns and the streets with the red and white flowers.

PAGE 124 crocuses

> *Ruy Belo, poet (1933–78), vocal in his opposition to Salazar. He believed resistance was intrinsic to the nature of poetry.*

This poem speaks as though Anaktoria might be in America at this time. It also seems to answer (or pose) the question of Anaktoria's being real or imagined—or possibly both.

PAGE 129 reach

singing, *see o nymphs what*

clear vision your tagus nurtures in its worthies,

A cutup of lines from the *Lusiads,* canto 1. Renata ends her book with words from the beginning of Camões's epic.

The title conjures a reach for a new beginning, if not a new world. Reach is also a sailing term. Wind in the sail from over the side of the boat is a beam reach, from an angle near the stern, a broad reach, and from an angle toward the bow, a close reach. With prevailing winds in Lisbon mostly from the north, Renata's skill (as I remember it) would allow her nearly a broad reach—good sailing.

As I write this, I can see the boat in the distance, its sail bellied, the boom, the gaff, battens, the halyard, the sheet. The three women look to me resplendent and fierce, not nymphs but possibly immortal in the moment. The boat, of course, is a weasel, green, with red and yellow trim.

The author of five poetry collections and two novels, Frank X. Gaspar's work has appeared widely in magazines and literary journals. He has held the Hélio and Amélia Pedrosa/Luso-American Development Foundation (FLAD) Endowed Chair in Portuguese Studies at the University of Massachusetts Dartmouth and currently teaches in the Graduate Writing Program at Pacific University, Oregon.